WAR AGAINST THE SCHOOLS' ACADEMIC CHILD ABUSE

Siegfried Engelmann

Copyright © 2020 (NIFDI Press)

All rights reserved. No part of this publication may be reproduced, distributed, or transmitted in any form or by any means, including photocopying, recording, or other electronic or mechanical methods, without the prior written permission of the publisher, except in the case of brief quotations embodied in critical reviews and certain other noncommercial uses permitted by copyright law. For permission requests, write to the publisher at the address below.

National Institute for Direct Instruction
P.O. Box 11248
Eugene, Oregon, 97440.
www.nifdi.org

Printed in the United States of America

ISBN: 978-1-939851-27-7

Library of Congress Control Number: 2018948121

Please note: This book is a reprint of the 1992 edition of *War Against the Schools' Academic Child Abuse*, originally published by Halcyon House. NIFDI Press has not edited the text. Consequentially, some organizations may no longer exist and individuals may be deceased. If you have any questions, contact info@nifdi.org.

CONTENTS

PERSPECTIVE 1
1 – THE REFORM CYCLE 9
2 – BASAL PROGRAMS 15
3 – THE FAINT VOICE OF REASON 25
4 – CALIFORNIA'S WHOLE-LANGUAGE INITIATIVE 33
5 – THE SUPPORTING CAST 45
6 – ACADEMIC CHILD ABUSE 59
7 – LET'S GO TO COURT 71
8 – EFFECTIVE TEACHING 83
9 – THEORIES 99
10 – MATH MADNESS 113
11 – GIVE THEM THE BUSINESS 133
12 – HOW SCHOOLS GUARANTEE FAILURE 153
13 – HOW TEACHER COLLEGES GUARANTEE FAILURE 165
14 – SYSTEMIC CHANGE 181
15 – HOW CAN WE GET THERE FROM HERE? 195
16 – YOU 205
    REFERENCES 217
    INDEX 225
    ABOUT THE AUTHOR 234

PERSPECTIVE

In the summer of 1966, the Anti-Defamation League expressed interest in making a film showing the achievements of the disadvantaged black preschoolers we had been working with at the University of Illinois. Two years earlier, these kids had been selected for the project as four-year-olds on the basis that they came from homes that were judged particularly disadvantaged and nearly all of them had older siblings in classes for the mentally retarded. These kids came to our school half-days as four-year-olds and as five-year-olds.

The school, The Bereiter-Engelmann preschool, received a lot of bad press. It was called a pressure cooker. Sociolinguists took shots at it on the grounds that we ostensibly did not understand "black English," or even know the difference between "thinking and speaking."

Despite our alleged mental deficiencies, we managed to teach these kids more and make them smarter than anybody else had done before or after. That was our goal, particularly with this first flight of kids – to set the limits, to show what could be done. We felt that this demonstration was particularly important because Headstart was looming in the wings, and it was clearly moving in a direction of being nothing more than a front for public health, not a serious educational project. We saw this as a great contradiction because disadvantaged kids were behind their middle-class peers in skills and knowledge.

We taught reading, language, and math to our preschoolers. And they learned these subjects. They also learned to learn well and therefore how to be smart. A film showing what these kids could do might moderate what seemed to be the inevitable mandate of the Office of Economic Opportunity to designate Headstart as a "social experience" based on the model of the middle-class nursery school. It seemed obvious that the model would not work.

We rounded up seven of the kids who were in our top group. (We grouped kids for instruction according to their performance.) They were in the middle of summer vacation, and we didn't have an opportunity to work with them before the film to "refresh" or rehearse them. A professor at the University of Illinois found out about the filming and asked if she could bring her class to view it. Why not?

Perspective

So seven little black kids came into the classroom, sat in their chairs in front of the chalkboard with big bright lights shining on them, with two big cameras on tripods staring at them, and with a class of university students in the background. And these kids did it. There were no outtakes, no cut sequences, nothing but the kids responding to problems that I presented, the types of problems I had taught them to work. These were not necessarily the problem types that one would present preschoolers as part of a 12-grade sequence, but they were good problems to show that these kids could learn at a greatly accelerated rate.

On the film, the kids worked problems of addition, subtraction, multiplication, and fractions. They worked problems in which they found the area of rectangles and problems in which they found the length of an unknown side of the rectangle (given the number of squares in the rectangle and the length of one side). They worked column-addition problems that required carrying and problems that did not require carrying. They even worked problems involving factoring expressions like 6A+3B+9C. And they used the appropriate wording: "Three times the quantity, 2A, plus 1B, plus 3C."

The kids told me how to work a simple algebra problem: "The man at the store tells you that ¼ of a pie costs 5 cents. You want to buy the whole pie. How much is the whole pie?"

After telling me how to work the problem by multiplying by the reciprocal of ¼, I wrote the answer as $20. The kids jumped up to correct my sign error, one boy observed, "Wow, you have to pay **that much** for a pie?"

And the kids did dimensional analysis involving the equation: A+B=C. They told me how to rewrite the equation so it told what A equals (A=C–B), what B equals (B=C–A), and what C equals (C=A+B).

The last problem type I presented on the film was the simultaneous-equation problem:

A + B = 14
A – B = 0

They had worked on similar problems in which A and B were the same size (inferred from A-B=0) and they quickly told me that the numbers were 7 and 7. There was still time left so I presented them with a brand new problem type:

A + B = 14

$$A - B = 2$$

I pointed out that when you start with A and minus B, you end up with 2. So A is bigger than B. They frowned; they thought; and finally, the little girl sitting on the end of the group – who is now an engineer – said in a wee voice, "8 and 6." These were kids who had not yet entered first grade.

The film made no difference in deterring Headstart from becoming a program that produced no real gains. Nor did it give notice that failure with disadvantaged kids was a failure in instructional practices. We had shown, however, that all the disadvantaged black kids we worked with could learn to read and perform basic arithmetic operations in the preschool and that the average IQ gain of these kids was 24 points.

In 1968, we moved into the primary grades by becoming a sponsor in the world's largest educational experiment, the $1 billion U.S. Office of Education Follow Through Project. Follow Through was supposed to be like a horse race, with various "sponsors" implementing their approach in different places and competing both with other sponsors and with the traditional Title 1 programs. We were called the "Direct Instruction" sponsor, and we designed and managed school programs in 20 different sites including large city schools (in New York City and DC) and rural areas (Uvalde, Texas and Las Vegas, New Mexico). From the beginning, the Follow Through game was clearly to identify winners and losers, to clear the air of rhetoric about what works and what doesn't, and to adopt successful practices.

Our competition consisted of 12 other major sponsors (each of which had more than two sites) and a lot of self-sponsored sites. The competition presented the range of prejudices of the day, which is the same range that is present today. Most of the sponsors were "child developmentalists" who rallied around theories like those of Piaget. There was the Open Classroom model that believed in the natural ability of children to make choices and intelligent decisions if given space and opportunity. There were projects like the Tucson Early Education Model that promoted "language experience" reading (which is all but identical to the "whole language" approach that is currently in vogue) and Cognitively Oriented Curriculum, which focused on social development. Some of the sponsors stressed "discovery learning," and problem solving of the type that is popular today.

Each sponsor went out with its prejudices and practices ostensibly to find out what works well. Working as a Follow Through sponsor was no fun for any sponsor because it brought people from the world of rhetoric and theories into blunt confrontations with schools. This reality check proved overwhelming for some sponsors and resulted in less-than-ideal implementations for all. Since Follow Through sponsors were selected by parent groups, the sponsor was often at odds with the participating school district. In some of our districts, the game was clearly to do things to foul up the implementation (not ordering instructional material on time, removing trained aides after the school year had begun, assigning misfit teachers to the project, imposing district guidelines for scheduling the health and safety program, the PE classes, and district mandated "social science," and consequently making it very difficult to schedule reading, language, and arithmetic).

We worked with over 9000 kids a year, which would be a large number if they were all in the same community and not spread out across the U.S.

In 1976-77, after Follow Through had processed a couple of waves of kids who started in kindergarten and went through the third grade of their designated approach, Follow Through was evaluated by Abt Associates in connection with Stanford Research Institute.

The results make a mockery of current reforms, because Follow Through clearly showed that some approaches work well and some flop; however, the ones that flopped the most emphatically are still alive today and still promoted vehemently by teachers' groups like the International Reading Association, the National Council of Teachers of English, and the National Council of Teachers of Mathematics. The approaches that did well were roughly the opposite of the romantic notions and theories espoused by these groups. The better performing sponsors presented highly structured instruction that had tight teacher-performance requirements and practices that are "behavioral."

The Follow Through results showed that the Direct Instruction model had soundly beaten the other competitors. Specifically, the kids in Direct Instruction who started in kindergarten achieved:

First place in reading;

First place in arithmetic;

First place in spelling;

First place in language;

First place in basic skills;

First place in academic cognitive skills;

First place in positive self-image.

In other words, our kids took first place in just about everything measured – first for urban sites, first for English speakers, and first for non-English speakers. Our non-disadvantaged kids in each site performed significantly above our disadvantaged kids and significantly above the level of non-disadvantaged kids in these same sites today.

Our disadvantaged kids performed near the 50th percentile (average) in the various subjects. The Title 1 program typically turned out kids who performed around the 20th percentile (which is 30 percentiles lower than we achieved). Some of the sponsors beat the 20th percentile, but most didn't. The ones with the sweetest rhetoric about children's self-image, discovery learning, and cognitive processes did the worst. Some had kids below the 15th percentile.

According to the promises of the Follow Through horse race, the big winner, Direct Instruction, was to now serve as the model for effective practices promoted by the Feds. Unfortunately, the concept of the horse race with winners and losers got lost somewhere between 1968 and the time for officially disseminating results about Follow Through. Heavy-duty lobbying efforts warned politicians against telling communities that their "child developmental" Follow Through model was a bust. After all, the parents loved it and thought it was great for their kids; the district loved it and didn't really care whether it was good for their kids so long as it brought in the federal dollars.

In the end, many sponsors were "validated" as being "effective," a practice that the Commissioner of Education, Ernest Boyer, opposed. He wrote, "Since only one of the sponsors [Direct Instruction] was found to produce positive results more consistently than any of the others, it would be inappropriate and irresponsible to disseminate information on all the models."

Not only was the notion of winners and losers warped by the dissemination efforts, there were active attempts to discredit our achievements in Follow Through, and even to suggest that sponsors like the Open Classroom model and the Language Experience model (Tucson Early Education Model) performed acceptably. The Ford Foundation arranged for two "analysts," Glass and House, to publish a report that played some incredibly bogus statistical games to discredit the Abt report.

After all these years, I'm still not sure I understand why it was so important for the establishment to discredit Direct Instruction. It's true that we do not do things the way they do it in traditional classrooms. But what we do works and what they do doesn't. If society is concerned with kids, it would seem reasonable to find what works and to use it, regardless of what our prejudices might be. If we don't rely on hard data, our prejudices don't have much to support them. Apparently, the key decision makers had a greater investment in romantic notions about children than in the gritty detail of actual practice or the fact that some things work well.

We survived the thundering silence that followed several esoteric debates about whether Follow Through actually happened. We watched what we had spent years cultivating in sites like Providence, RI, and Smithville, TN, revert to the weed patch from which it sprang. We saw the districts we had worked with erase their memory banks and look to new theories about child development.

We next focused on older kids who had failed; we developed various instructional programs, including videodisc programs for teaching math and science. Our format for developing programs involves first figuring out what works well, then incorporating these practices into lessons. This format is quite different from that of the typical commercial instructional program, which is created in sterile isolation from children's behavior.

We also established a unique Ph.D. program at the University of Oregon. The program assumes that the most essential middle-management position in a school district is a trainer who has the skills needed to be a demonstration teacher and implement effective training and monitoring practices. Typically, school districts operate without such a position, which is the system's primary flaw – one that renders it incapable of serving children effectively.

During the years that I've worked with kids and teachers, I have never seen a kid with an IQ of over 80 that could not be taught to read in a timely manner (one school year), and I've worked directly or indirectly (as a trainer) with thousands of them. I've never seen a kid that could not be taught arithmetic and language skills. During these years, however, I've become increasingly intolerant of reforms formulated by naive spectators who don't really understand what school failure is and how it can be reversed. The curriculum (the instructional programs and the details of how kids are taught) is the difference between failure and success. The difference is not a "global" aspect such as "cooperative learning" or "discovery." The difference has to do with what the kids are doing, how they are using what they have been taught, and most important, how they receive specific skills, facts, and operations that they are to use in applied situations. When the curriculum fails, the teaching will fail. Period. This is not to say that if an excellent curriculum is in place, the teaching will automatically succeed. It means simply that the curriculum is like an automobile. The teacher's behavior is like driving that automobile. If the car is well designed, the teacher has the potential to drive fast and safely. If the curriculum is poorly designed, it will break down no matter how carefully the teacher drives.

Broadly framed reforms about "upgrading" teachers by paying them more or by finding "smarter" teachers are absurd. The teacher is a teacher – not a genius, an instructional designer, or a counselor. The teacher must be viewed as a consumer of instructional material. The material must be shaped and tested the same way any other important product would be. Unfortunately, that is not the way it is done in education. The public doesn't know it, nor does the business community. Both are frustrated with the schools, but they don't know where to begin to achieve "reform," and they are easy targets for any reformer who gives an articulate description of the problem and then offers a non-sequitur solution. Parents, as Secretary of Education, Lamar Alexander, has said repeatedly, are poor judges of how well their kids are doing in school. In many cases, however, it is not their fault: the schools have lied to them by redefining what reading is or by providing them with "choices" of educational formats (as if parents are knowledgeable about what the different "choices" really imply).

The system panders and plays games because it is thoroughly incompetent at the top. The decision makers have a dual character of being naive and arrogant. They are naive because they have never taught successfully, or even seen it done. They are arrogant because they install practices that are totally untried and subject thousands of kids to certain failure.

This book does not go into great detail about how we teach kids reading, arithmetic, or whatever. Instead, it concentrates on the functional problems with the system, why it is guilty of academic child abuse, and what you can do about it. The basic theme is that the teachers are largely victims of incompetence at the top. To change education so it can work for all kids does not involve experimenting with new formats of interaction or providing for national assessments as much as it involves cleaning up the administration so that decisions are responsible. Classroom practices must be monitored and responded to in a timely manner. Key decision makers must be judged by their deeds, not their rhetoric. Those who have a history of making decisions that lead to kid failure should be labelled as failures and either put out to pasture or sent back to the factory to receive a thorough overhaul. The demands that should be put on administrations are pretty simple:

- Don't install instructional approaches unless you KNOW that they work well;
- Don't permit textbook publishers to market product that have not been tried out with a single kid before or after publication;
- Don't permit lobby groups with the loudest voices and the biggest budgets to promote practices that amount to nothing more than the *opinion* of the group;
- Don't permit practices that are not working acceptably to remain in place for years without responding to the failures of teachers and children;
- Don't respond to failure of a "reform" by blaming the children, their homes, the changing demography, or some other irrelevant factor.

If these *don'ts* were adopted, the academic child abuse and unnecessary failure that characterize the current educational scene would be eliminated in three or four years.

In the following chapters, I'll try to explain the games that schools and educators play. You may find much of what I present difficult to believe. However, it's easy to test my assertions by going to the nearest school.

CHAPTER 1
THE REFORM CYCLE

No doubt exists about the incompetence of the U.S. educational system. Its failure is documented almost weekly with new studies and reports showing how poorly U.S. students perform compared to students in Japan, Hong Kong, and even in some cases, Canada. Kids who can scarcely read graduate from high school. Knowledge deficiencies in science, history, and comprehension are the rule, not the exception. Graduate programs in math and the hard sciences (physics, chemistry) are dominated by foreign students in just about every major university. Typically, less than a quarter of the students are home-grown kids, and typically the natives are hanging on, not excelling.

Our kids are our future, a fact that the informed public recognizes and that the educational system refers to in its rhetoric. The existence of such pandemic failure in the schools, therefore, seems to be a horrible contradiction. Our nation is relatively wealthy; our middle class relatively well informed and concerned about their kids. So why does such incredible failure exist in the schools? It certainly doesn't seem to be genetically possible for successful, intelligent parents who went through college in the '50s and '60s to have children and grandchildren who perform so poorly. It doesn't seem plausible that our social environment could have changed so much over the past 30 years that today's kids are incapable of learning. Nor does it seem reasonable that the new curricula have been affected by the "information explosion" to such a degree that reading and arithmetic are incomprehensible to the young mind.

Educators, sociologists, and psychologists provide many explanations—the changing demography in the schools (with larger representation of minorities), breakdown of the traditional family structure (with possible traumatic consequences) and basically anything else that has changed over the past 30 years. But these are largely weak explanations, based on correlations. They don't really explain why

Chapter 1: The Reform Cycle

Fred and Martha Anderson were successful in a rigorous college environment and why one of their grand kids does well in school (gets good grades) but lacks very basic knowledge, and why their other grand kid is a third grader who carries the labels of "dyslexia" and "learning disabled."

The bottom-line conclusion is obvious. For whatever reasons, the schools are a categorical failure. The schools are our agency for training kids in skills that are assumed to help them in later life—primarily by providing them with choices. A kid who can't perform rudimentary mathematical operations by the eighth grade is all but preempted from a future in physics, engineering, or medicine. An eighth grader who can't read on the third-grade level probably will not become a lawyer, a doctor, or possibly even a clerk in an automotive parts store. The extent to which the schools fail to teach kids the basic skills that are assumed by higher education is the degree to which the schools fail. Our schools have earned a grade of F.

Although the bottom line is perfectly obvious, the cycle of reform is not. This cycle represents a contradiction because the reform is often fashioned by educators (or those on the periphery of education). Furthermore, once a reform has been adopted, who implements it? The educators.

Both aspects of the cycle are contradictory. What reason do we have to believe that the people who fashion these reforms know what they are talking about? Usually there is very little evidence in the credentials of the founders. The proposed reform is usually based more on hope and rhetoric than on fact. And why should we believe that educators are capable of implementing the reform even if it is sound? The people who become charged with implementing reforms are the same folks who are responsible for the incredible failure of our kids. They have demonstrated no technical expertise in teaching kids, in training teachers, or in organizing schools so they are effective.

The premise of this book is that the problems in the schools exist because of ignorance about what can be done with kids (versus what is being done). The main proposition is that so long as we remain ignorant and permit the schools to be directed by people who are obviously incompetent in the instructional arena, our kids will continue to be second- or third-raters. The problem is not confined to one or several aspects of the educational system. Rather it involves all the higher-echelon parties—educational publishers, boards of education, teacher-training institutions, school administrators, the funding agencies (the Feds, primarily) and the educational press. Together, these segments guarantee failure.

Teachers are part of the problem, but they are largely victims. Most elementary school teachers have never received training that would permit them to succeed with all kids. Many have never even observed an excellent teacher. The general incompetence of teachers can be documented by the performance of their kids. When fifth graders can't do problems that involve division, their failure is prima facie evidence that the teaching failed. If the teaching failed, the teachers failed. But the teachers did largely what they were told to do, or permitted to do. And the people responsible for telling them what to do are a large part of the problem.

Why was teacher **A** hired when it was evident that she knew nothing about managing kids or presenting instructional activities? The schools are responsible for this part of the kid failure in the classroom. Why was she able to graduate and receive a teaching certificate if she was so grossly deficient in basic teaching skills? The college of education and the state certification board seem to be culpable on this issue. Why was she permitted to use a math textbook that had never been demonstrated to work well in teaching kids? The textbook publishers and their license to publish untested, unsound programs is implicated on this issue. Also, the textbook-selection committee that adopted the textbook is responsible.

Why wasn't the teacher's performance monitored by the administration, and why wasn't she either trained or fired? This issue involves the school's administration and its interaction with the union. The administration clearly fails, but why doesn't the board do something about it? The board is largely concerned with fiscal issues, donating less than ten percent of its time to instructional matters and no time to monitoring the administration to assure that administrators perform duties ordered by the board. Instead, the board usually demurs to the "expertise" of the administration on matters of instruction, of selecting

Chapter 1: The Reform Cycle

materials, and of providing in-service "training" for teachers. Instead of directing, the board is actually directed.

Just as the administration and the school board are obviously guilty of in competence, they, like the teachers, are victims. The administration must frequently follow regulations and guidelines provided by state and federal funding agencies. The details of these regulations are typically naive, because although they may have been proposed through sensible legislation, they were translated by educators.

The system is sick because the vast majority of people in it—from educational researchers to teachers—lack technical understanding of the single aspect of the schools that justifies their existence—instruction. The administration knows frighteningly little about it; teachers are far less knowledgeable about it than you would imagine; even educational publishers, whose business it is to provide instructional material, are not literate about instruction. In businesses like supermarkets, management trainees become well versed in all aspects of the store before taking over decision-making roles. Not so in education. Administrators typically know little more about teaching than the bookkeeper. Nor does the Peter Principle apply to education. People are not elevated to higher positions because they excel at a lower-status level. Probably the exact opposite is true. Excellent teachers do not share the establishment's beliefs and folk lore. They frequently represent a threat more than a resource. The aphorism, "build a better mousetrap and people will beat a path to your door," holds in other fields, but not in education. There is a negative correlation between effective programs in elementary schools and the programs schools use. Because decision makers in education are not knowledgeable about instruction, they are suckers for any theory, any barrage of rhetoric that "seems plausible" or that presents the right words.

Nobody is to blame, but unless the sickness is recognized—soon—and unless something helps the institutions get well, the system will not improve. Reforms will come and go, but they will fail. The establishment will continue to provide rhetoric that appeals to our patriotism, our love of children, and other romantic notions, while the system's deeds continue to contradict its rhetoric. True reform will occur only when informed citizens become educationally literate and place demands on schools, Feds, publishers, and colleges of education to put their actions where their rhetoric is.

The expression, "What goes around comes around," does not apply to education today, because there are no "stoppers" within the system—no segment that marks where the buck will stop, no segment with solid knowledge about what is reasonable. The trends over the past three decades have clearly demonstrated that in education what goes around simply goes around, until it runs out of gas. The new math came and it went, leaving teachers, parents, and kids with a bad taste in their mouth. The disadvantaged were bused from here to there and back, and the performance of the schools dropped to a new common denominator. The humanistic emphasis of the '70s resulted only in teachers teaching less and suggesting that it was more significant. New trends follow old ones. When a trend fails, the educators simply deprecate it, offer a new solution, and the press presents it as some new breakthrough in learning or understanding.

To stop this insanity and to create an educational system that is scientific, sound, and product oriented—with the kids being the product, and the reduction to zero of damaged merchandise the goal—there is only one possible stopper, which is an informed public. Unfortunately, the informed public is far more informed about Neptune and the ocean floor than it is about the schools. In fact, the more people read about education, the more they become indoctrinated by the theories and approaches that are at the heart of the schools' failure.

CHAPTER 2
BASAL PROGRAMS

Let's say that we were going to create an instructional program, and let's say that we are reasonably intelligent and that we have some concern for both the teachers and kids who use the program we develop. It would help if we knew the subject that we were trying to teach. The more we know about it, the more likely it is that we'd be able to take the first steps of laying out a sequence of activities for the teacher to follow. It would also help if we had some knowledge about how kids learn, but this knowledge is not really necessary if we use our intelligence.

After we lay out a series of activities for teaching the subject, we have a choice. We can either say, "We're done. The program is completed, and it will work," or we can try out our rough-draft product in the classroom. We'll choose the latter alternative because we have some concern for the kids, and we're not arrogant enough to assume that the sequence we created in the sterile confines of our office will automatically translate into lively, effective instruction in the classroom.

So we arrange for a couple of teachers to try out our program. Again, we have to make a choice. Do we just let the teachers do their thing and report back to us, or do we observe what actually takes place in the classroom? Being cautious, we choose the latter alternative again. After all, the teacher is going to have her hands full working with the kids. She may not remember everything that's important, or she may be poor at reporting details.

In any case, we observe our program in action. As observers, we have to make another choice. Are we going to judge that our program is acceptable if **some** of the kids perform well on it, **most** of the kids perform well on it, or **all** of the kids perform well on it?

This decision is thornier than the others because we know that there is a range of individual variation in the classroom. But after mulling over the criterion problem for a while, we decide that all the kids who have skill levels high enough to be placed in the program should perform well—which means learn everything the teacher teaches. We realize that they may miss occasional items, but we don't want them to miss bunches of items. So we work out a kind of formula for what percentage of errors on each item represents an acceptable performance for our program.

Observing the field tryout of the program may test our personal commitment and our ego. We put a lot of time into developing the program. Obviously, we think we did a pretty good job. (If we didn't think this, we'd still be working on the program, not trying it out in classrooms.) But we may still feel very insulted when we observe what happens. Chances are, we'll find out that the teacher has all sorts of mechanical problems presenting the material in an appropriate way. Even when she presents it in a manner that we judge to be acceptable, the kids may make a lot of mistakes. Probably the whole program will appear to be a disaster.

Another decision. Do we assume that we're just working with bad teachers and bad kids (which would still leave us with the illusion that our program is pretty good) or do we take responsibility for the problems of the teacher and kids? Let's say that we're thick-skinned enough to endure the insult of our failure (particularly since we see just about exactly the same pattern of behavior in each classroom we observe).

We have to redo our program. This time, we have more to go on than we did before. But how do we interpret the errors in a way that will help us revise our program? Since we're taking on the task of creating an excellent program, the interpretation is straight-forward. The errors are information. If errors occur in a pattern, the pattern shows us exactly what we did that was wrong. If there are a large number of errors on an item, we know that the "teaching" we specified that preceded the item was inadequate. In other words, the precise identification of the problem implies the solution. This important principle might not occur to us immediately, but as we work on trying to correct errors, we most probably will discover it.

Once more we select a couple of new classrooms and observe our revised program. This time, the performance of the teacher and kids looks a lot better, so much better, in fact, that the boo-boos in the revised program stand out like islands in the ocean. Fortunately, there aren't enough to warrant a total overhaul of what we've done. Since we're right there in the classroom watching the teacher, and since we're now pretty good at interpreting the mistakes the kids make as information about where our program is weak, we're able to give the teacher revisions the next day to take care of most of the problems we observe.

However, there are still "lumps" in our program, rough places where the teacher talks too much, where the kids go off task and get confused. and where the presentation seems labored or too easy for the kids. When we finally work these lumps out, we have a good program, one that we can say with confidence will work in classrooms that have kids like the ones we've been working with. (By now, we've seen a very consistent pattern in performance, with the teachers' and kids' performance paralleling the refinements of our program.)

In addition to having a good program, we have a great deal of knowledge about how kids learn and how to teach well. We know how much practice it takes for the kids to master the various details of our sequence. Oddly enough, the amount of practice that we've had to provide to meet our goal is possibly five times the amount provided in other published programs that teach the same subject. We have also learned that kids tend to "lose" information if we don't keep it "alive" in the program. This observation had led us to activities that require kids to use all the important skills and concepts they've been taught. We've learned that teachers do a better job of presenting material when they move faster, and that long explanations are anathema. We've found out that the best way to assure that teachers don't blow the presentation completely is to script it—write down the exact words the teacher is to say. And the pattern of interactions that works best is a short explanation followed by a series of questions that kids answer out loud. Their responses provide a good test whether they have adequately received the intended information.

Possibly the most important lesson that we've learned from this experience is that the kids' mistakes are just about always reasonable. Kids sometimes misinterpret what the teacher was trying to communicate, but their misinterpretation is absolutely consistent with what the teacher did and showed. The lesson about the lawfulness of kid performance may have come to us slowly, because it's a difficult one, particularly since we already know the concepts that the teacher is trying to teach. It's difficult to look at the instruction through the kids' eyes. However, the patterns of mistakes the kids make provide us with overwhelming evidence that when kids "mislearn" something, their misinterpretation is consistent with what the teacher did or said.

Although our initial goal was simply to develop an excellent program, the field-tryout process has taught us a great deal about motivation, "psychology of learning," "communication ambiguity," and about the subject we thought we knew. The mistakes the kids made forced us to sharpen our knowledge of the subject, look at the details far more closely, and look at the subject from the standpoint of the naive learner.

If you developed a program in this manner, the chances are excellent that it would be received by the traditional educational community not with open arms but with open mouths that delivered slanderous rhetoric. Educators would actually have the audacity to suggest that your program was not "consistent with the way kids learn." They would say that it stifles creativity, that it is too structured, that it is not based on an understanding of the subject, and just about any other negative comment you could imagine. Of course, the traditionalists wouldn't have first-hand knowledge of how the program works and what it does, because "educators" do not deal with the concrete. For them, issues are general. They wouldn't understand, for instance, that if you developed a math program that taught "borrowing" or "regrouping," you'd have to address many "subtypes" of problems.

Borrowing for this problem

$$\begin{array}{r} 376 \\ -\,182 \\ \hline \end{array}$$

is quite different from borrowing for this problem

$$\begin{array}{r} 386 \\ -\,189 \\ \hline \end{array}$$

or this problem

$$\begin{array}{r} 300 \\ -19 \\ \hline \end{array}$$

For educators, issues of specific detail do not exist. Their concern would be expressed by questions, such as "Does the program teach real math applications, rather than focus on mere skills?" If you developed a reading program, the concern expressed by educators would not be with the details of the program and whether it works. Instead, the concern would be with much broader issues such as the tired controversy between "sight reading" and "phonics."

For the traditionalist, the boundaries between good and bad are marked by large categories, and therefore, by half-truths. Phonics works better than sight reading. But that doesn't imply that all phonics programs are good. It all depends on the details of the program. Traditional educators express opinions through metaphysical arguments that revolve around the categories they understand; but the real issues—those that make the difference between a program that works and one that flounders—are very picky, precise, technical matters. The difference between the first field-test program and the finished product you developed is simply gritty detail, not global goop.

Following the development of your program, you would discover that you did not speak the language of traditional educators. Your language would be much closer to that of the teacher who tries to teach well, because that teacher is capable of comprehending the level of detail you use. The college professor and educational researcher isn't (with few exceptions).

Even more distressing, you'd find that you had very little common language or understanding with the publishers of traditional programs. The reason is that commercial programs are not developed the way you developed yours. You had to make a decision following your desktop first draft. You could have said, "I'm done. The program is completed and it will work." Although you were neither arrogant nor stupid enough to suppose that it would be done at this point, the commercial publisher (almost without exception) is. Commercial programs used by schools—your schools—for teaching reading, language, arithmetic, science, and social studies are not field-tested before publication. They are not shaped by learner and teacher problems. They are simply made up by people who know no more about excellent instruction than the typical copywriter or graphics designer.

It is difficult to imagine how we could have such elaborate "field-testing" of drugs, appliances, gadgets, cars, and other consumer items but have no counterpart in education. As a friend of mine once said, "A bottle of aspirin tells the dosage and the dangers; yet, we don't have any similar statement for instructional programs—even though most of them are much more dangerous than any non-prescription drug." The Surgeon General issues all sorts of warnings on cigarette packs, but unfortunately, we don't have a Surgeon General for instruction.

How are the basals produced? The commission on reading for the National Council of Teachers of English, under the direction of Dorothy Watson, put together a tedious document titled *Report Card on Basal Readers* (the sight-reading basals that had been the overwhelming favorites of school districts). Although the report is replete with naive interpretations and conclusions that could fill a book of "false dilemmas," the commission does a reasonable job of detailing the typical steps involved in developing a new basal reading program. Here's a topic-sentence summary from the *Report*:

> "The company calculates what the current market is, how many companies share this market and what potential share a new program could get."
>
> "Next, the company estimates the cost of producing the program..."
>
> "Now the publisher develops a product strategy. Which segment of the market is the program intended for?"
>
> "The next step is to decide the physical characteristics of the program with the marketing personnel again taking the lead but with the cooperation of editorial and art representatives."
>
> "Only then is the company ready to begin considering criteria for content. And this again involves market analysis."
>
> "Publishers... wait to see which terms and concepts pop up in their competitors teacher's manuals."

"Next, the publisher gets a target date for publication."

"Almost the last thing that happens in developing a plan… is choosing the authors, who may not even be involved in any of the plan's development."

"How much of the actual writing the authors will do is a variable from series to series… Publishers generally find that they control the time, content, and quality of writing better when it is done by people employed by them as editors."

"Most editors are not highly paid… Editors, like teachers, work from their own intuitions about what is best for the pupils… Unlike teachers, however, they do not have any feedback from a group of learners. They could, of course, arrange with nearby schools to try out materials with kids. That's time-consuming and rarely done in any systematic way."

"Though publishers work hard to include a range of selections written by well-known children's authors, most of what eventually winds up in the pupils' anthology is either adapted or specially written for the purpose."

"Most of the material in the kindergarten and first-grade levels is written by staff members… Starting often in second grade and beyond, most of the material is from literature already published for children but it is adapted."

"The first step is adapting to fit the readability and skill criteria of the publisher."

"During the process of editing the series, there is a continuous… re-editing of the selections."

"Ironically, with all this passing back and forth of the story, it is rare that children are brought into the process for their reactions or reading. In fact, the books will almost always be in print before a child has an opportunity to respond to it and it is only if teachers report these responses that they may have an impact on subsequent revisions."

I've added the emphasis in the last paragraph above to make the point that the typical basal is an experiment, and not a very noble one. The chances are just about zero percent that programs developed in this manner will work well, even if those involved in the creation are very knowledgeable about the subject matter. Unfortunately, most editors are not excellent teachers; they are English Lit or Journalism graduates who happened to learn some rules of grammar and punctuation along the way.

Even the authors of "award winning" children's literature often know very little about kids. Consider those who concluded that these works were worthy of awards—people who have probably never gone through the detailed process of actually finding out what kids like, what they can actually read, and what kinds of problems they have if instruction for particular skills is not very careful. These people are not responding to what **kids** like; they are expressing what **they** like.

I know three people who write for major basal publishers. Each receives assignments, much like the assignments that are provided to an artist. Each receives an outline, a statement of how long the piece is to be, and possibly some criteria about the "vocabulary," and sentence length. All the people I know who do this are smart, good writers, and very punctual; three attributes that are highly valued in the basal business. All agree that the process is criminal, leading to series that are terribly fragmented and ill coordinated. One of them told me, "I just won't work on programs for very young kids. I feel that I can't do a lot of harm with the older kids, but I wouldn't want to be responsible for screwing up young kids."

I seriously believe that the reason basal publishers do not shape their products through field tryouts is that they don't know how to do it, and they don't really care. They are in the business of making money. If school districts are naive enough to buy a particular basal in sufficient numbers to make the product profitable, publishers feel that they are successful. They don't have to answer to Nader or any other consumer-advocate group. They are not inspected by the Feds. Their programs are not reviewed and graded. Instead, they are placed on the open market.

Organizations like the NCTE pose as "advocates." Their endorsements purport to be motivated by concern for teaching all kids effectively. Actually, documents like the *Report Card on Basal Readers* is a con that has three parts. The first is the exhortation to improve practices for the sake of children; the next is an elaborate description of the problem; the third is an endorsement of an unproven method for teaching kids. The con is apparently very effective because endorsements by these groups typically lead to large-scale adoption of practices by school systems. The decision makers are apparently so mesmerized by the statement of commitment and description of the problem that they conclude, "How could anybody with all this commitment and knowledge provide a solution that is less than enlightened?"

Indeed the NCTE *Report* provides example after example of how publishers had rewritten classic stories and reduced the prose to simple, stupid sentences in attempts to satisfy "readability" formulas for controlling vocabulary. The Report documents that the worksheet activities presented after students read a story often have nothing to do with the story or anything else in the lesson. The report mentions the problems with the "multiple choice" format of items that test whether kids learn such things as "main ideas." The format is artificial at best. Nobody says, "Which of the following summaries would you suggest best describes the passage you just read: A) A woman became good friends with a donkey, B)..., etc? And the *Report* documents possibly the biggest problem of all, which is that the basals do not promote actual reading. Possibly ten percent of the time schools schedule for reading instruction is devoted to reading.

Finally, the NCTE endorses a practice that will ostensibly solve all these problems: **whole language**.

Whole language is based on the questionable notion that language is a whole and that learning to read will happen if you just immerse kids in language. Part of the immersion involves writing down what the kids say or selecting a piece like *Jack Spratt* and going over it with the kids ad nauseam until they have memorized it. Because children memorize the material, some derive classic misinterpretations of what reading is supposed to be. They suppose that you first have to "discuss" something before you can read it. They think that the reading is nothing more than a strange recitation game, during which you must point to the words in order and slowly recite the familiar sequence of words.

While some kids may learn to read from this approach (nothing is preventing them from learning what they're supposed to learn), some higher performers may totally misinterpret the game, and lots of lower performers fail to catch on to what reading is.

We once did a nice demonstration that showed how confusing the approach may be to naive kids. We went into a first-grade classroom where a teacher had worked on four different selections. Each had an illustration and the text. The kids could "read" all selections perfectly. We then switched the illustrations (paired them with different texts) and tested the kids. About half of the kids pointed to the words one at a time and, with great fidelity, recited the passage that was appropriate for the **picture**. In other words, half the kids didn't have the faintest idea of what reading was all about.

As part of the endorsement of whole language, the *Report* concludes that teachers should throw out basal readers and teach without them, using literature. The basals are seen as an evil that deprives reading specialists of their right to make instructional decisions.

There are several problems with this solution: The first is that teachers are typically slaves to instructional programs and follow them very closely (even when they tell others that they don't). The second is that there is no evidence to support the assertion that typical reading specialists are capable of designing instruction that is effective (and a lot of data to suggest that they aren't). The third and most serious problem is that a reading specialist who designed even one grade-level of a program that worked well with the full range of kids, would have to work on it no less than 6 hours a day for a minimum of two years.

CHAPTER 3

THE FAINT VOICE OF REASON

Shortly before the publication of the *Report* by the NCTE, another report stirred up reading educators. This document, *Becoming a Nation of Readers*, reviewed the host of studies on teaching reading and arrived at the conclusion that the best way to teach beginning reading is through careful phonics instruction. The report, published in 1985, was a joint effort of the National Academy of Education, the National Institute of Education, and the Center for the Study of Reading at the University of Illinois. Because the report was a committee effort, it has some fluff and nonsense in it and it tends to take a less-than-assertive stand on some issues; however, it was the first major-league report that emphatically supported the practices that we use in the reading programs we have developed (MHE's *DISTAR Reading Mastery* and *Corrective Reading*).

We teach explicit phonics, the sounds of individual letters and letter combinations. The report concluded that "The trend of the data favors explicit phonics."

We teach oral blending skills. The teacher says a word like man slowly, "mmmaaaaannn," directs the children to say it slowly, and then to "say it fast." The report concluded that blending activities facilitate learning to read.

To teach comprehension skills, we use direct-instruction techniques. The report observed that, "There is evidence that direct instruction produces gains in reading achievement beyond those that are obtained with less direct means such as questions."

The theme that emerges from *Becoming a Nation of Readers* is the antipode of the NCTE endorsement—although both make the same observations about the problems with traditional basals. While the NCTE report suggests that there is no need for formal reading programs (just use *Junior Classics*), *Becoming a Nation of Readers* stresses the need for careful instruction. "Teachers of beginning reading should present well-designed phonics instruction."

Chapter 3: The Faint Voice of Reason

The NCTE report is obsessed with the fidelity of the "literature" and the language that appears in the beginning readers. *Becoming a Nation of Readers* is concerned with the fidelity of beginning **instruction**. For instance, "Reading primers should be interesting, comprehensible, and give children opportunities to apply phonics. There should be a close interplay between phonics instruction and reading words in meaningful selections." If this recommendation seems strange, it is because many basals are strange. They provide for the teaching of "phonics," and then present readers that don't contain words the kids can read by virtue of what they've been taught about "phonics."

In microcosm, the NCTE report and *Becoming a Nation of Readers* illustrate one of the most serious problems with education, which is: Who do you believe? Here, both operate from the same information base about the problems, but their solutions are dramatically different. They even refer to some of the same data, such as the fact that New Zealand uses whole language and New Zealand has the "highest" literacy rate of any nation. For the NCTE, this fact is sufficient evidence. For *Becoming a Nation of Readers*, this fact is an inconsistency.

> It is noteworthy that these approaches are used to teach children to read in New Zealand, the most literate country in the world, a country that experiences very low rates of reading failure. However, studies of whole-language approaches in the United States have produced results that are best characterized as inconsistent. In the hands of very skillful teachers, the results can be excellent. But the average result is indifferent when compared to approaches typical in American classrooms ....

The approaches used in the average American classroom produce an inexcusably high rate of teaching failures. To do no better than these programs is to perform at a level that has led to calls for reform.

There are serious problems in using New Zealand as the sole data base for an instructional approach. The first is that the demography of New Zealand is quite different from that of New York City or Denver. The second is that the conclusion about New Zealand being the "most literate" country in the world is based on the performance of 18-year-olds in school. New Zealand has a strict tracking system. Only about 15 percent of the population is in school at age 18.

A general rule in education is that approaches adopted by school districts are usually not based on facts, but on philosophy. The confrontation of whole language and the recommendations of the *Becoming a Nation of Readers* is consistent with this general rule. While *Becoming a Nation of Readers* made little impact on schools, publishers, or decision makers, the whole-language movement became a sweeping trend, spurred largely by the state of California's incredible initiative to mandate whole-language for all kids.

Ironically, publishers have developed whole-language basal series that teachers can use to teach the various language arts, and these programs were developed in exactly the same way the NCTE judged as being inappropriate for the development of "look-say" (sight-word) basals. Publishers started with the same projections, went through the same rewriting, and came out with programs that had never been field-tested with a single kid before being put on the market and purchased by schools. Since there is no strong data to support the whole-language approach, why did it become so popular? The answer seems to be: it appeals to educators. The appeal comes largely from the supposition that learning is somehow natural if the teacher uses whole-language and artificial with material that is organized.

A trio of writers (Bess Altwerger, Carol Edelsy, and Barbara Flores) explained the "natural" properties of whole language in an article published in *Reading Teacher*, which is the official publication of the International Reading Association.

> The key theoretical premise for Whole-Language is that the world over, babies acquire language through actually using it, not through practicing its separate parts until some later date when the parts are assembled and the totality is finally used. The major assumption is that the model of acquisition, through real use (not through practice exercises), is the best model for thinking about and helping with the learning of reading and writing.

Chapter 3: The Faint Voice of Reason

> Language acquisition (both oral and written) is seen as natural—not in the sense of innate or inevitably unfolding, but natural in the sense that when language (oral or written) is an integral part of functioning of a community and is used around and with neophytes, it is learned "incidentally"...
>
> ... Little use is made of materials written specifically to teach reading or writing. Instead, Whole Language relies heavily on literature, on other print used for appropriate purposes (e.g. cake-mix directions used for really making a cake, rather than for finding short vowels), and on writing for varied purposes.

Here's a summary of the argument, stripped of rhetoric:

1. Written language is language.
2. Babies acquire language through actually using it, not through practicing its separate parts.
3. Oral language is learned "incidentally" (as an aspect of doing something else).
4. Therefore, written language is best learned "incidentally" (à la the cake-mix routine).

This argument represents metaphysics at its worst.

In the first place, written language is **not** language. It is a representation of a language, hopefully of a language known to the learner. Linguists (real linguists) universally agree that if there is no talking, there is no language. As Ronald Langacker put it in his book, *Language and Its Structure*, "Language is speech and the linguistic competence underlying speech. Writing is no more than a secondary, graphic representation of language..." Furthermore, the material the kids learn to read is based on a very specific language, not just any old language. Most of us wouldn't talk in English to English-speaking kids and then, as part of our whole-language activities, present written French. The fact that we recognize that practice as being insane indicates that the written language kids learn is based on thousands and thousands of things kids have already learned about their spoken language. We don't start from scratch when we teach reading. We assume a base of oral-language understanding.

The next problem is the assertion that babies don't practice separate parts when learning language. When they start out babbling, what language is that? Also, the fact that a six-year-old knows a lot more language than the two-year-old suggests that many specifiable "parts" and aspects were learned. Also, what's happening in a situation when a mother says, "Can you touch your nose? Nose?" The kid does it. "Oh, you remembered how to touch your nose."

Is this a language activity? It seems to be one, but the **kid didn't say anything**! The mother did all the talking. And the activity did seem to deal with a discrete part or skill. Just ask the mother. She'll assure you that the baby couldn't do it three weeks earlier.

The next problem is the argument about incidental learning. The writers assure us that when oral or written language is used around neophytes, it is learned "incidentally." It is a natural occurrence. The problem is that reading written material is not much like most oral-language exchanges. If we were to present oral-language activities that parallel reading activities as closely as possible, the oral-language activities would go some thing like this.

Parent:	Say this: We are having fun.
Kid:	We are having fun.
Parent:	Say this: You are a smart girl.
Kid:	I am a…
Parent:	No. Say **you**. **You** are a smart girl.
Kid:	You are a smart girl.
Parent:	Now you've got it.

Also the analogy between the baby learning language and the six-year-old learning to read is pretty limp. The six-year-old has already mastered the language. She is able to follow instructions. She knows much about word meaning and syntax. Because of her sophistication, the teacher is able to **direct her learning**. That learning is quite specific. It does not involve learning a language but a code for expressing a familiar language. Typically, the instructional setting doesn't involve one mother and a baby but one teacher and possibly 28 kids. So, the teacher can either entertain herself by baking a cake

Chapter 3: The Faint Voice of Reason

(or possibly 28 of them so that all the kids are actively involved) or she can use efficient means to teach kids the very specific things they don't know about "written language."

The person who may be most responsible for the whole-language movement in the U.S. is Kenneth Goodman, past president of the International Reading Association. Goodman has been around for years, using his conception of linguistics to pose as an advocate for the underdog—the disadvantaged, the non-English speaker.

He and his wife, Yetta, wrote a paper, "Twenty Questions About Teaching Language" that is often quoted by whole-language advocates. I believe that their response to this paper shows that whole-language advocates are not very critical readers. Here's an example from the Goodmans:

> Early in our miscue research, we concluded that a story is easier to read than a page, a page easier than a paragraph, a paragraph easier than a sentence, a sentence easier than a word, and a word easier than a letter. Our research continues to support this conclusion and we believe it to be true.

Here's a "rational" refutation. How could the kid read a sentence without being able to read the component words? If the words are harder than the sentences, and if the sentences are composed of words, what phenomenal kind of linguistic gymnastics permits the kids to transcend the more difficult unit (words) to get to the easier unit (sentences)?

Here's a pragmatic refutation: Most of us know how hard it is for a kid to "read" a letter like **B** or **J**; the Goodmans assert that it is much, much easier for the kid to read a story. There is something seriously wrong with this picture.

Another pragmatic refutation: If something is harder than something else, there's a greater probability that somebody would fail to learn it. If the Goodman "hierarchy" of difficulty is accurate, we would expect to find some kids who have what might be called the "Goodman Syndrome." These kids would fluently and accurately read stories, but when asked to read a page, they would tend to make more mistakes. These kids would stumble miserably over individual words and would have incredible trouble following directions to identify individual letters. I've seen lots of kids who have reading problems, but never one with the "Goodman Syndrome." Have you?

Naturally, the Goodmans argue against the idea that kids should learn to read accurately.

> It is through the errors… that we've learned that reading is a psycho linguistic guessing game… The Hawaiian child who reads "He was one big fat duck" for "He was a big fat duck" is letting us in on the ability to read one kind of dialect and translate into dialect in order to comprehend.

My response is to consider the first part of the poem, *Trees*, by Harry Befin:

Trees are the kindest things I know,

they do no harm, they simply grow.

And spread a shade for sleepy cows,

and gather birds among their boughs.

Now consider how one of Goodmans' word guessers might read it:

Trees are the kindest things I know,

they do no harm, they simply grow.

And spread the shade for drowsy cows,

and collect birds among their branches.

Can you imagine Goodmans' word guessers trying to put on a play from a script? Let's hope that the script contains nothing in dialect (even Hawaiian dialect).

The Goodmans have a quaint way of dealing with the facts about reading instruction. They simply deny the facts.

> …we can teach children letter names and the sounds letters represent and we can teach them words in isolation from the context of language, but we know that these methods do not lead children to reading.

So much for all the studies that show the superiority of phonics.

Chapter 3: The Faint Voice of Reason

Possibly the most fascinating aspect of arguments presented by the Goodmans and other whole-language advocates is that nobody laughs at them.

An obvious reason for accepting such stupid arguments is that they handsomely serve educators. The whole-language "reform" requires exactly no professional responsibility from teachers, because there is no bottom line; there are no downside contingencies; the possibility of failure or need for plan B is not even an issue. The process is "natural."

The credulous teacher who provides the choice, the flexibility, and who encourages the "integration" the Goodmans demand discovers that a third of her little guys can't read—although the Goodmans assure us that learning will take place. The teacher has met all the requirements for "natural language development." The only possible conclusion is that those kids who didn't learn have something wrong with their natural processes, or they just aren't "ready."

The kids get blamed for the teacher's failure. However, traditional educators have a way of transforming failure into success. One way is to say that our expectations for kids reading by the end of the first grade is unreasonable because many aren't "ready" and the children need more time to play and develop before "formal" instruction begins. Another approach is to redefine literacy.

A fourth-grade teacher who had been using whole language with lower performing kids told me this: "My kids just love books. Of course, they can't read, but they love them."

That teacher probably gave the best of all possible reasons for the wholesale acceptance of whole language. It provides an infinitely elastic standard that transforms obvious failure into success: "My kids just love books."

CHAPTER 4
CALIFORNIA'S WHOLE-LANGUAGE INITIATIVE

The state of California played a large role in the rapid adoptions of whole language. California has a state-wide textbook adoption process which is required by the California constitution. According to the constitution, the State Board of Education is to adopt textbooks for use throughout the state in grades 1-8. A large segment of the California educational code has statutes that clarify the adoption process. A state Curriculum Commission assists the board by constructing all the material that is needed for the adoption. The Curriculum Commission develops standards, organizes review panels to process the material submitted by publishers, and makes adoption recommendations.

The State Board has been illegal for years. The first statute in the part of the education code that deals with adoptions starts out by saying, "At least biennially, the State Board shall adopt..." The board doesn't adopt programs biennially. The Board's cycle, like that of some locusts, is about every seven years.

The statutes are replete with language about adopting programs that promote "maximum efficiency and effectiveness of pupil learning." One statute provides for the Board working with publishers to improve learner verification–the documentation that the adopted programs actually work well with kids. But this statute became law in 1976, so it was probably premature to suppose that the board could have acted on it in anyway by the 1988 adoption.

The scene in California was fairly grim at the time of the 1988 adoption. The business community was voicing serious complaints about the quality of students graduating from high schools. The demography of the state was changing. Over half the kids in schools were minorities. The average performance of kids was far below the national "average." The state Superintendent of Public Instruction, William Honig, was busy fashioning reforms, ostensibly with full knowledge of what he was doing. As he stated in 1985, "I don't think

Chapter 4: California's Whole-Language Initiative

you can be an instructional leader unless you have some concept of what the instruction, the curriculum is all about." If the details of the California adoption reflect Honig's concept of the curriculum, people in California need instructional leaders like Honig about as much as they need another earthquake.

Before considering the California approach to adopting programs, consider how an intelligent instructional leader might go about it. First, he'd get some facts about what works, particularly with non-English speaking kids, other minority kids, and low performers. (After all, the average kid in the state is a low performer.) As part of the search for information, the leader would identify teachers who consistently do an exceptional job. With the thousands of people employed by the State Department of Public Instruction, the leader should be able to find a work force that could go through achievement scores in selected districts and find the teachers who consistently produce superior results (those higher than teachers of comparable kids). Next, the leader would arrange interviews with superior teachers and find out what they do, what type of materials they use, how they teach, and whom they would recommend as being "expert" in training teachers or implementing instructional approaches.

Finally, and long before mandating any solution on a state-wide basis, the instructional leader would **field-test** the proposed plan to discover precisely what kind and how much training was needed, and how the plan worked in tryout situations.

How many of these steps did California's instructional leader take? None.

Instead Honig, the Department of Instruction, the State Board, and the Curriculum Commission proceeded with great confidence in the opposite direction. Without field-testing, the state formulated curriculum frameworks, standards, criteria, and compiled support documents to promote the pre-determined thrust of the 1988 reading adoptions—whole language.

I was interested in the California adoption for several reasons. We had worked with various districts in California and we were concerned that the new guidelines would effectively shut down successful implementations in places like Carlsbad, Del Paso Heights, Monterey, Portersville, and Bakersfield. Another reason for my interest in California was that the *DISTAR Reading Mastery* series was submitted for adoption.

The programs are submitted to the Curriculum Commission and are first reviewed for "legal compliance," to make sure that the series doesn't promote such evils as sexual bias, the use of alcohol or drugs, racial stereotypes, or violation of safety rules. If the submission fails the test of "legal compliance," it's out of the running. Next, the program goes through a content evaluation, during which three different panels evaluate the program against the standards and criteria adopted by the State Board. The content review results in a score. The Curriculum Commission then recommends the programs with "passing" scores to the State Board, at a public hearing. The adopted programs are made available to the schools at a special rate out of a specified category of the school budget. Although it is possible for districts to request a waiver to use programs that are not on the state-adopted list, most districts don't like to exercise this option because it represents going against the grain. So most use their allotments to purchase the adopted programs.

Even before the Curriculum Commission had finished evaluating programs, the California School Leadership Academy (an agency that provides training for administrators) put on a workshop to train administrators in the state's new initiative—whole language and teaching reading through literature. One document in the workshop packet was *Building a Quality English-Language Arts Program*. Pages 96 and 97 present a checklist of "What you shouldn't see in a classroom." One of the items on page 97 is: *Skill kit work—SRA, Distar-Type kits.*

The only thing **like** SRA *DISTAR*-type kits **is** SRA *DISTAR*, which means that the Curriculum Commission's evaluation of *DISTAR Reading Mastery* may have been a mere ritual.

Panel 9 reviewed *DISTAR Reading Mastery* for legal compliance and came up with 24 pages of citations, covering nine categories. Most of the citations were incredible, but possibly the most outrageous was this pair of juxtaposed observations about Level 3 of the program.

> "Whole book limited to Caucasian and Black characters."
>
> "P. 22 and 23 Story and Illustration: stereotyping of Indians—not all had canoes."

While dealing exclusively with Caucasians and Blacks, we managed to stereotype Indians. For what it's worth, the first sentence of the story on page 22 begins like this: "Not all Indians use canoes, but ...."

On appeal, *DISTAR Reading Mastery* made it through legal compliance. The next hoop was the three-panel evaluation for content. According to the Curriculum Commission's policy manual, the primary qualification for the evaluators on these panels is "subject matter expertise." Also the panels are supposed to "show a balance of male and female participants." The Commission interpreted these procedures by assembling panels composed of garden-variety teachers—the type that could be found in any average-performing school. The gender balance of the panels was 29 females to one male.

In March of 1988, the evaluators were "trained" in procedures for evaluating instructional programs. The opening address, or keynote, came from Dr. Marilyn Buckley (an assistant professor at the University of Alaska).

Buckley gave a melodramatic eulogy of whole language, featuring such quotables as, "The *Framework* is not asking for a new curriculum. The *Framework* is asking for a new teacher," and "Unless we change the curriculum, (the teacher) will never be free." I'm not sure where anybody got the idea that the teacher should be "free," but apparently that is a popular position.

Buckley's pedagogy is consistent with the Goodmans'. When discussing procedures for introducing new reading selections, she cautioned, "Do not allow the vocabulary to be introduced beforehand." Buckley likes to surprise the kids rather than prepare them.

One of Buckley's most curious comments had to do with the role of "literature."

> The purpose of literature is to please the human spirit. It is not to allow us to teach oral language. It does not exist for us to set up the writing program...

> Literature is there… for the human spirit, for the human soul, to be enlarged, to be enriched.

After wiping the tears from our eyes, we might consider a perplexing question: If we give this description of literature the benefit of many doubts and accept it as valid, why would we choose literature as the core of a program that is supposed to teach reading, writing, and oral language? Buckley's prose seems to contradict the idea that literature is a reasonable vehicle for such teaching.

On the subject of publishers, she suggested that the evaluation process may be a formality. "We want to stand by and support… every publisher who has been moving in concert with the best that we know about language. The others—will just have to go back to the drawing board."

Following the opening address, the evaluators had a fun-filled agenda, which included observing a real live "whole-language" lesson, in which fifth graders discussed the fable, "The Man, the Boy, and the Donkey."

Perhaps the most necessary part of the training was to acquaint the evaluators with the way the programs were to be "scored." The details of the scoring may give you a headache because it involves reweighting favored criteria and requires an advanced degree in "busy-work." The form for evaluating the student material contains criteria grouped into seven different categories. The categories: literature, comprehension, skills development, style and structure, organization, assessment, and student's study material.

Within each category are scoreable criteria. The evaluator examines the program, and rates it on each criterion, from 1 to 5 (1 for a poor showing, 5 for a super showing). Then the evaluator "multiplies" each score by the "weighting factor" for the criteria. Different criteria have different weighting factors. Most are x1 or x2; several are x4; and one is even x5. That category, of course, is the quality of the literature selections in the program. After the weighting, the evaluator **divides by** the total multipliers to get something of an average for each of the seven categories.

The cycle is then repeated. The **average** score for each category is subjected to another multiplier. (Literature is multiplied by 5, but no other category has a multiplier of more than x2.) After dividing by the total of the multipliers, the evaluator has an "average" score for the program; however, this average is now greatly distorted by the weighting and reweighting. It would be like starting with seven glasses, each half-filled with water, adding different amounts of sugar to different glasses, then pouring off the excess so that each glass was still half-full. (By the end of the reweighting, the analogy may be a little weak because you wouldn't be able to pour the excess from the glass that corresponds to "literature"; you'd have to spoon it out.)

With this weighting procedure, one of the 24 scoreable criteria—quality of the literature selections—is worth 25 percent of the total score, and one of the seven categories—literature—is worth 35 percent of the total score. For whatever reason, the evaluation called for one more "averaging," this time a "holistic score" for each of the seven categories (1 through 5). This score was averaged with the first and possibly demurred the outrageous weightings provided by the first cycle of averaging.

Several points seem obvious. The first is that the people who devised this preposterous reweighting scheme must have had experience working for small loan companies or automobile dealerships. They should be placed on the consumer-beware list. The second point is that the weightings provide hints about California's instructional leaders and the slogans that drive their reasoning. Two criteria had weightings of x4, suggesting that these were pretty important criteria. Here's one:

> (The program) Guides students through a range of thinking processes (e.g., evaluating, comparing, concluding, inferring, analyzing and summarizing) without using a hierarchical approach (i.e., assuming that students must acquire one type of thinking before being able to deal with another type).

Notice the stipulation that the program shouldn't use a hierarchical approach. Common sense would suggest that some things are harder than others and that a sensible program would start with the easier material and progress to the more difficult. In the list of thinking processes, for example, are concluding and summarizing. According to the criterion, you could present kids with the task of summarizing an argument that draws a conclusion without first teaching kids something about identifying conclusions and how they work. Amazing.

The incredible ban about hierarchical approaches seems to come from the Goodmans. In their paper, "Twenty Questions," the Goodmans reject "hierarchies."

> No research has produced any information to suggest a reader must know this letter, this sound, this word, or this syllabic rule before some other.

The fact that no research has produced such a "natural hierarchy" (and hopefully never will) is irrelevant. This conclusion is a lot like saying, "There's no single natural way to build automobiles; therefore, we should randomly throw parts together." The notion of a natural hierarchy for reading is absurd because reading is a "taught" skill, not one that ever develops outside the context of teaching. The letters and words on the page don't give the learner feedback. They don't sing out, "Wrong," if the kid says the wrong sound or wrong word. They just sit there, and without intervention from someone knowledgeable about the code, no learning would take place. Since some sounds and some inflections don't occur in all languages, it's even more ridiculous to talk about a natural hierarchy. If there were one, French kids, Japanese kids, and U.S. kids would learn to speak the same words, the same sounds, in the same order.

Although a natural hierarchy is unattainable, it doesn't follow that programs should be un-hierarchical. The question is not whether a program is based on a "natural" hierarchy, but whether the earlier-taught skills in each program prepare the kids well for the skills taught later.

Finally, I'm not sure how a program could be designed so it didn't assume a hierarchical approach. One way might be to provide the teacher with a system for generating random numbers. Before each lesson, the teacher could select the random lesson (or random pages) for the day, open the book and launch into non-hierarchical teaching.

Chapter 4: California's Whole-Language Initiative

In all, the California selection criteria are pathetic. Some criteria imply empirical knowledge and cannot be applied simply by "examining" the program. Yet the evaluators are supposed to make armchair judgments on items like these:

> (The selections engage students in) Works that stimulate active response and provide enjoyment; Works that stimulate an interest in language in both the receptive and expressive forms.

How does the evaluator judge the selections if she has never seen the effect they have on kids? Adult judgments don't always correspond to kid judgments. As a very good teacher in Turlock, California put it, "If you really want to bore the shit out of a classroom of fourth graders, treat them to a dramatic reading of *Bambi*."

The evaluation of *DISTAR Reading Mastery* by the three panels resulted in 102 comments, most of which are negative and factually incorrect and some of which are just plain dumb.

Panel C found a serious problem with selections in the third level of the program that dealt with ancient Troy.

> "In Reading Mastery 3, ...there are four tales from the Aeneid, not written in their original forms."

In the first place, they are not based on the Aeneid (which presents only one of the legends–the Trojan horse). In the second place, I'm not sure that the program would have been greatly improved if we had presented the material in its original form, Ancient Greek.

Panel C judged:

> "Limited direct instruction is provided for comprehension strategies."

The DIS in *DISTAR* stands for Direct Instruction System. We **invented** Direct Instruction, and *Becoming a Nation of Readers* cited research on our teaching format when concluding that comprehension skills should be taught through direct instruction.

Panel B observed:

> "Many selections were content area related, especially in the areas of science and social studies."

Isn't the basic game to teach kids how to read and "seek meaning"? If it is, then the areas of science and social studies would seem to be primary targets for reading instruction. Kids are often totally unprepared for such reading; yet this reading is supposed to occupy much of their academic time.

None of the panels recommended the program for adoption. The "holistic summary" of panel A provides the general flavor of the consensus:

> The SRA Reading Mastery series is a skill-based reading series which contains very few examples of good literary works and these literary works are at the fifth and sixth grade levels only. Stories for the lower grade student texts are chosen for readability only and contain no pieces worth literary merit. The program does not teach writing as a process and has no writing activities for students at the lower grades and only four sentence paragraphs at the fifth and sixth grade levels. It is a lock-step process that is devoid of activities involving teacher or student creativity as stories are read and workbook pages are filled. The SRA Reading Mastery Reading Series addresses very little of the new English-Language Arts Framework in its design, choice of reading selections, and its approach to involving students in reading, writing, speaking, and listening.

From that description, you wouldn't get the impression that the program has been involved in scores of comparative studies and has consistently won. You certainly wouldn't get the idea that *Reading Mastery* and its associated research had six references in *Becoming a Nation of Readers*, that it has been judged by American Institute for Research in Behavioral Sciences (AIR) as an exemplar in its series, "It Works," or that analytical studies of reading programs, such as those that had been conducted by Isabelle Beck, rated the program excellent in continuity of skill development. You certainly wouldn't believe that it had been mandated by court order in two different California districts.

Naturally, we appealed the decision. Steve Osborn, who co-authored levels 5 and 6 of the program, appeared before the Curriculum Commission and refuted the various assertions. He observed that, "Of the 102 statements made by the panels, 73 are factually incorrect." He presented the Commission members with a 20-page single-spaced rebuttal.

How did the Commission respond to Osborn's rebuttal? The appeal was rejected. Dan Chernow, a Commission member who works in some branch of television, not education, pointed out the incredible flaws in Steve's rebuttal by referring to a story in the first level of the program. It was not "literature." And all other matters were unimportant if the program was not literature based. It's rejected. All done.

The California adoption process is largely a charade, but the most frustrating aspect of it is that nobody calls the Commission on its inaccuracies, misinterpretation of data, or absurd criteria. Readers of the state's propaganda are apparently so immobilized by the magnificent appeals that they couldn't check out some of the references.

One section of California's *Language-Arts Framework* (the state's blue print for its curriculum mandates) opens with what seems to be a quote from *Becoming a Nation of Readers.*

> Recent research indicates that students benefit from instruction that makes explicit the strategies being used to promote comprehension in reading. The climate is right for growth when the learner becomes the center of the learning rather than the teacher and when the thinker discovers that "thinking needs to be made public" (i.e., when the teacher explicitly teaches strategies for synthesizing and integrating information, and when students are not left guessing as to how to comprehend ideas). (cited in *Becoming a Nation of Readers*, p. 72)

The only part from *Becoming a Nation of Readers* is the part in parentheses. The rest—all that business about the thinker discovering that "thinking needs to be made public"– is an adaptation, at best. Here's the original:

> Research has shown that children's learning is facilitated when critical concepts or skills are directly taught by the teacher. The section on phonics in the preceding chapter concluded that breaking the code is easier for children when instruction directly provides information about letter-sound relationships. Similarly, comprehending information in textbooks is easier if students are instructed in strategies that cause them to focus their attention on relevant information, synthesize the information, and integrate it with what they already know. Children should not be left guessing about how to comprehend. In the words of one researcher, "Thinking needs to be made public."

The *framework* also provides "teaching suggestions." The one I like best tells how to teach spelling.

> (The students) only spell when they write, and the only words they need to know how to spell are the words needed in writing; therefore, one of the best instructional strategies is to generate students' spelling lists from their writings.

This is what is known as brain-dead logic. If we use this recommendation for individuals, we are not preparing them with the "only words they need to know how to spell," because we don't know what words are needed in their **future** writing. We could, of course, have them repeatedly write the same thing they just wrote; then they would be well prepared with the "only words they need to know." If we make up a spelling list based on words the entire class uses, we're violating the notion of **who needs these words**. I think it's fair to say that individuals need their own words, unless the entire class engages in synchronized writing, in which case, the first sentence should read something like this, "The class only spells when it writes, and the only words the class needs to know how to spell is the aggregate of words the class needs." Either version is pretty dumb.

CHAPTER 5

THE SUPPORTING CAST

During the 1988 California adoption process, I wrote a lot of letters. When the California School of Leadership Academy came out with the assertion that you shouldn't see *DISTAR* in the classroom, I wrote letters to find out the data base for this judgment. Several went to Fred Tempes, Assistant Superintendent of Instruction. I asked Fred to provide answers to two questions:

1. Where has the state field-tested the procedures being promulgated by the Department of Education?
2. What data does the state have that the program works as well as *DISTAR*?

I pointed out,

> Certainly you must have performed comparisons before making the determination that *DISTAR* is something one wouldn't want to see in a classroom. And, certainly, your decisions must be based on DATA. Please specify the data basis for this conclusion…

Does it come as any surprise that Fred never really answered the question, that he didn't send a list of places where the state had done its homework? Fred's project liaison did respond to a letter from an SRA representative who objected to the reference about *DISTAR*. Here's what she had to say about the role of The California School Leadership Academy:

> While I can appreciate your point of view, the reality is that the State of California has adopted Frameworks, Curriculum Guides, Quality Criteria, Review documents, materials and assessments which focus on this approach. The California School Leadership Academy training program helps school principals to focus on their work realities which are impacted by state expectations. And although CSLA does not promote only one right answer, we do feature a particular viewpoint.

Chapter 5: The Supporting Cast

And there you have it, a summary of the educator's way of solving problems. You start with the particular viewpoint, then launch into the production of materials to promote that viewpoint. You merchandise that viewpoint through the overwhelming repetition of your theme.

The workshop packet that principals received for their training by the California School Leadership Academy is an example of the end product. The 250-page packet contains scads of articles that illustrate the California "viewpoint."

One article, written by Judith Langer, professor of Education at Stanford, provides a splendid example of what traditionalists often call "research." They conduct a study in which nothing is taught. Instead, they "study" something about the kids' behavior. They then suggest teaching techniques that are based on what the kids do. This kind of "study" gives no indication of what caused the kids' behavior in the first place. To demonstrate that the behavior is "natural" and inevitable, the "researcher" would have to show that the behavior is stable regardless of the instruction the kids receive. Because traditional researchers don't show that, their studies are basically irrelevant to teaching.

Langer investigated "comprehension," and she apparently worked with kids who were pretty deficient in "comprehending" what they read. Here's, apparently, the most Langer could milk out of their performance:

> I was able to show that after students finished reading a text, they rely on their final envisionments when they discuss and answer questions about what they have read.

I suppose this means that after you finish reading a who-done-it or a story with a surprise ending, you'll have a different impression of the work than you did before you read the ending.

The Langer plan, based on this revelation, is to have students complete a work and then answer very special questions. "After reading Romeo and Juliet, for example, a question like, 'How did you feel when Juliet decided to take her own life?' would be a place to start. Other questions to ask would be, 'What were you thinking at the end of the play?' or 'Why do you think the play ended as it did?'"

Following these splendid openers are questions that are more specific and "that move students back toward earlier envisionments." Some examples are: "Why do you think Juliet decided to take her own life?" or "What clues from the text made you think she would do it?" And so forth.

> These questions can be followed by personal experience questions such as, "Can you think of any experience in your own life that helped you better understand Juliet's predicament?" or "Is there anything you have read or have personally experienced that helped you understand how the play would end?"

As you may have observed, Langer's "technique" involves using "broad" questions. "None are minute questions about limited items of information that are not critical to an understanding of the text as a whole." In other words, no details about plot, characters, interactions, comparisons of customs, and perhaps most important, the specific wording of the text – line by line. So a 13-year-old girl commits suicide over a lost lover. Or possibly, her age is unimportant.

This formula for comprehension doesn't teach kids anything about how to read and interpret the work. It is simply a demur to kids' deficiencies. Possibly more distressing is the notion that details don't count. A significant work is nothing but details, arranged so that a very large percentage of them are significant. It would seem to be a travesty to gloss over the subtleties of lines like: "One fairer than my love? The all-seeing sun ne'er saw her match since first the world begun."

How does Langer's formula apply to other forms of reading—like a science text or a thoughtful essay? Understanding the text as a whole involves answers to "minute questions." Langer doesn't deal with such prosaic issues. She assures us, however, that her "…meaning ladened approach to reading instruction can also help us build a community of increasingly more critical readers and thinkers." I certainly don't know how, especially if kids are reinforced for remembering only the details that could be presented in a nine-sentence synopsis of the work.

Since we are not interested in kids who have only global understanding, we shouldn't use these kids as models for what we teach.

Chapter 5: The Supporting Cast

That would be like finding out-of-shape students and using them as the ideal end product of an athletic program. Sit down, Judith.

A lot of articles in the workshop packet deal with LES (limited English speaking) kids. The reason is that California has devised a unique approach for teaching them. But first, a dandy little article by Karen Galeano, titled, "Mother Goose in the ESL Classroom."

The article provides suggestions for the elementary grades (which typically go through grade 5 or grade 6). So when reading what Karen is to say, think of Juan, a "limited English" student (who actually knows almost no English) sitting in the fifth-grade classroom.

The article begins with a paradoxical argument that pleads for meaningful language, "The need for meaningful language in meaningful context is well documented in LES literature." The conclusion: "In choosing meaningful language for use in the LES classroom, one can do no better than to use a popular old standby. Mother Goose."

The advantages of Mother Goose:

> The Mother Goose rhymes tell a story; something happens in them that is interesting to children; the rhymes adhere to most of the principles that Oiler (1983) says a good story should have: surprise value (e.g., Peter, Peter Pumpkin Eater), interesting characters (e.g., Jack Spratt), meaningful conflicts (e.g., Little Miss Muffet), action (e.g., Humpty Dumpty), and they relate to the real world of the students they are aimed at (e.g., Mary had a little lamb).

I think Karen Galeano missed her calling. Anybody who could find so much literary value in these rhymes could teach calculus by using a stick and a pile of dirt. Remember the opening statement about the need for meaningful language in a meaningful context. What could be more meaningful than "Mary had a little lamb"? Since most of the children have lambs that follow them to school, the significance is obvious. Also, consider the remarkable character development of Jack Spratt, and the surprise value of Peter, Peter Pumpkin Eater would really knock the socks off a fifth grader, particularly the part about being able to keep her well in a pumpkin shell. (One might think she'd have some trouble surviving.) There's more.

> The Mother Goose stories provide springboards for discussion of a variety of skills… Mother Goose rhymes are an important part of our culture, and as such should be taught… Mother Goose is a basis for jokes, puns, and allusions in adult literature. Most of all, Mother Goose has been enjoyed by children since 1697. That is really standing the test of time.

Now for some of Galeano's pedagogy:

> When a child has a chance to comment on a poem, and his words are written by the teacher and shared… two things happen. First, the child realizes the value of what he says. His words are important enough to be shared with his classmates. He becomes a "published author." Second, he can go back to his words and read them… or pretend to, if he can't read yet… he knows that these marks on the paper represent what he said. This is written language and has meaning.

Galeano's kids apparently "love books." I wonder if they "love books" as much as kids who don't "pretend" to read. This would make an interesting whole-language study.

Galeano's approach involves using the rhymes as a point of departure for teaching everything in the universe. First, the rhyme:

> *There was an old lady who lived in a shoe.*
> *She had so many children, she didn't know what to do.*
> *She gave them some broth without any bread.*
> *And whipped them all soundly and sent them to bed.*

For "vocabulary development" the teacher is directed to a tangent involving shoes:

1. Kinds of shoes: slippers, high heels, cowboy boots, loafers, sandals, hiking boots, etc.
2. Where you can go in these shoes: beach, rodeo, dance, school.
3. What you can do in these shoes: dance, hike, ride a horse.
4. Parts of a shoe: sole, heel, toe, tongue, laces, buckle.
5. Categorizing: magazine pictures of shoes can be used to put the shoes into categories: Men/women/both, formal/play/work.

Chapter 5: The Supporting Cast

> 6. People names: There was an old man, lady, gentleman... who lives in a shoe.

For speaking-writing-reading:

> Teacher can ask, "Would you like to live in a shoe?"

For crafts:

> Make two cut-outs of a shoe and a bunch of cut-outs of children..., etc.

It's interesting that Galeano's tangent involves shoes and not something like whipping or the diet the old lady provides her kids. Which brings up an interesting question of legal compliance. Programs have been zapped by the legal-compliance panels in California for things like not portraying a balanced diet. But what about the cruelty of the old lady who lived in a shoe? She keeps getting pregnant. Does she blame herself or her partner? No. Instead she gives her kids a prison diet and beats them. Nice lady. But here's another thorny question. By virtue of what sort of logic does "literature" have immunity from "legal compliance" in California? Galeano's Mother Goose format is advertised as applying to all elementary grades, including grade one. Does the LES first grader understand that whippings and starvation diets are all right when something is labelled "literature" but that anything modern must ooze only goodness and cooperation? Or is what's good for the goose also good for Mother?

It's easy to make light of Karen's suggestions, because they're preposterous to the point that one has questions about how California could actually distribute that drivel. On the more serious side, it's a shame that Karen has never had an opportunity to at least observe effective instruction with LES kids (which obviously hasn't happened, or she wouldn't make the assertions she makes). It's even more disturbing that some unfortunate principals and administrators in the state of California are going to pass Karen's suggestions onto their teachers. But the most unfortunate is Juan, who can't ask the question, "How do I get to the 7-11?" in English, and certainly can't answer it. Instead of learning "meaningful language in a meaningful context," he is treated to an old woman who lived in a shoe.

One of the heavier articles in the workshop packet is written by Mary Barr, "Implementing a Research-based Curriculum in English-Language Arts, K-12." For the state, this article is important because it apparently is California's substitute for first-hand knowledge or field-testing. The article is a study in propaganda, making references to *Becoming a Nation of Readers* and generally pretending that there is a research base for the California plan. Another objective of the article is to set the stage for the notion that all kids – from learning disabled and LES kids to the gifted – are to be taught **in the same classroom**, using the same material.

Mary plays the whole-language game of citing research of the type that Langer conducts, quoting somebody's **opinion** but presenting it as fact, and liberally misquoting or stretching a point far beyond the context in which it was presented.

For example, in discussing comprehension skills, Barr presents this summary:

> In summary, skills are by-products of the whole act of making sense out of experience. Skills develop naturally when students write and speak in order to be understood, read and listen in order to understand. The studies cited below provide testimony.

I suppose in all fairness, Barr doesn't indicate what the studies provide testimony to. In the list that she presents are a couple of fluff studies, but also *Becoming a Nation of Readers*, and a study by Isabelle Beck ("Effects of Long-term Vocabulary Instruction on Lexical Access and Reading Comprehension"), which presents an orientation that's roughly opposite to the one Barr is promoting.

On the issue of phonics, Barr quotes someone named Bussis et al. who acknowledges "the correlation between reading success and knowledge of phonics," but who explains that it "is reading for meaning that causes children to learn to use phonics." That's Bussis et al's opinion. Why not quote Al Grossman, the neighborhood electrician? Al has produced as much research to prove his point as Bussis et al. has. The reader, unfortunately, doesn't understand that Barr isn't "proving" her

Chapter 5: The Supporting Cast

point, but is merely name dropping. The reader may not recognize gossip when it is presented in the meaningful context of et als.

Once writers like Mary get into their stride, they can produce single para graphs that contain at least half a dozen misstatements or half-truths. Consider this one:

> Second language learners, learning disabled students and disadvantaged students are the ones who can least benefit from the mechanical skill-based approach to language learning because it contradicts their own experiences and erodes their confidence in their abilities to make sense. The contradiction is especially damning now that research has documented so convincingly the common ingredients for all students if they are to develop linguistic and academic proficiency: they must connect what they need to know to what they already know and they must focus on meaning in what they are reading and writing.

All the students named in the first sentence have been shown to learn more in less time from "skill-based" programs. That doesn't mean that all skill-based programs will achieve this goal. Some are stupid. So far as the skill-based approach eroding confidence, this assertion (like the first) is flatly contradicted by much research. Again, it is possible to design a skill-based program in which kids fail. Failure will certainly make students less than confident in their ability to "make sense." Mary's universal formula (making connections and focusing on "meaning") seems to have a missing ingredient, which is how this connection is made. How do kids connect what they need to know if they don't know the concepts or skills that serve as anchors for the connections? Neither the anchors nor the connections are possible without teaching. How many unfortunate ninth-grade non-readers have been conned by some misguided teacher who thought that the kids would learn if only they were interested and motivated to make connections? Armed with the highest-interest material they could find, these teachers launched into "reading instruction" but didn't get past first base in the "Sports" series or out of the pit stop in the "Race Car" series. Without the missing ingredient of careful teaching to forge the links between what the kids know and what they need to know, Mary's little formula flounders.

If we taught swimming according to Mary's formula, we would do away with beginning swimming classes and replace them with intermediate "activities," which would include beginners and even possibly people who have serious physical limitations. Then we would engage in swimming – not skills. Everybody swims – perhaps playing water polo. If occasional kids drown, it certainly wouldn't be our fault. All the kids had to do was connect what they needed to know to what they already knew. They knew they'd be playing water polo, so...

Mary Barr's article sets the table for what has to be the most outrageous paper in the packet. The article, "Equity and Access in a Language Arts Program for All Students," should be enshrined in the Propaganda Hall of Fame. This paper, written by Phillip Gonzales, is so bad that it almost makes Goodmans' arguments seem sensible.

Gonzales' major theme is that all kids must have access to the same core curriculum, which to Gonzales prompts the one and only possible conclusion: that all kids – from gifted to LES must be placed in the same classroom.

Gonzales asserts: "Upon entering the **exemplary** English-language arts classroom, a visitor would immediately be struck with the activities." (I suppose this is a metaphor and does not suggest violence of any sort.)

> All students are studying the same piece of literature and the intent is to help all students derive meaning from the lesson. The piece is challenging for most in the class, including the "gifted" as well as engaging for the English-as-a-second-language students. Yet, such students are not singled out for separate instruction. Students are not identified by supposed "giftedness," or educational disability, cultural... background, or primary language.

In the average "middle-class" fourth grade, there is a range of ability from about first-grade level to eighth. In a class like the one Gonzales described, the range of difference is probably from pre-kindergarten to seventh, with the average kid performing around possibly

Chapter 5: The Supporting Cast

mid-second-grade level. The teacher, bristling with wisdom and magical power, is going to present selections that challenge the gifted and engage the LES kids. Perhaps, as you think about Juan sitting in this classroom, you are curious about the nature of these selections. Remember, Juan is sitting next to a disadvantaged kid who can't read a second-grade primer accurately. On the other side is Jennifer, who reads on the seventh-grade level.

The format of lessons, of course, involves literature. The program is loose and discontinuous, because there is apparently very little need for careful organization or teaching.

> The student, in understanding literature and in creating his/her own texts, employs all of the language arts skills of reading, writing, and speaking. Each does not need to be taught separately nor in any presumed sequence... The teacher, no longer viewed as the translator of the world for students, is now able to motivate and facilitate a generation of new ideas, conceptualizations, interpretations, and evaluations, among all students.

Imagine, reading does not have to be taught "in any presumed sequence." Possibly, this pronouncement is related to the notion that a story is easier to read than a page. So apparently, any selections would be reasonable for Juan's classroom, just as any selections would be appropriate for the first-grade classroom.

Gonzales' lessons begin with pre-reading preparation (and his description begins with a sentence that has a dangling participle). "Realizing that all literature is understood only as the student has a background to make sense of it, all lessons begin with a review of pertinent experiences and prior knowledge related to the content of the literature to be studied."

> Important issues, historical frames and other background information useful in helping students prepare for the lesson are... explored with students. In *Charlotte's Web*, students discuss a barnyard and the animals, the country fair, and the nature of fables. In *The Night Thoreau Spent in Jail*, groups of students research and discuss issues related to the Spanish

American War, such as "Manifest Destiny," Spanish colonialism, and the Monroe Doctrine…

Is there an incongruity of Juan sitting there, not able to identify common objects in English, and yet being meaningfully engaged in "Manifest Destiny"?

Gonzales suggests that there may be a problem. "Success in school tasks is dependent on whether students already possess knowledge related to the topic studied and whether they consider the lesson useful and meaningful." In other words, Juan is in deep trouble because he doesn't have the background knowledge. Gonzales, however, is not prepared for this conclusion, so he argues that Juan may not have trouble on the other grade-appropriate activities the teacher presents.

> On some topics, there are individuals who are able to perceive relationships more easily than others. In other lessons, these same individuals may have difficulty understanding and interpreting new content. Thus, individuals may be well-prepared for some school tasks, but not for others. Every student at some time exhibits characteristics of ill-preparation, and, at other times every sign of competence.

Possibly this passage should be given to teachers as a kind of screening test. If they fail to see the flaws in it, don't hire them.

I sincerely doubt that the teacher can construct any activity involving "the search for meaning" in which Jennifer doesn't outperform Juan. Consider the vocabulary words in *Charlotte's Web*. On page 114 of the Harper Trophy edition of the book, these words appear: **pasture, gander, anxiety, attraction, regular, radiant, befriended, reputation, terrific, slightly, breathe,** and **audience**. How many of these words do you suppose Juan can decode? How many do you think he understands?

Or, perhaps, some sentences, such as this one from page 123:

> *In the hard-packed dirt of the midway, after the glaring lights are out and the people have gone home to bed, you find a veritable treasure of popcorn fragments, frozen custard, sugar-fluff crystals,*

> *salted almonds, popsicles, partially gnawed ice-cream cones, and the wooden sticks of lollypops.*

Indeed the prose is colorful, and Jennifer is having a ball. But Juan is in a quiet kind of hell, the kind many of us would be in if we had to spend hours listening to mathematicians discuss functions in several variables or listen to a Portuguese-speaking teacher discuss anything.

According to Gonzales, Juan will learn from the other kids in the classroom:

> ...when less proficient writers and readers interact with other more competent writers and readers, they learn to more effectively use those reading and writing strategies already employed by their more successful peers.

Gonzales contends that the same thing happens with language:

> English becomes normal and natural for the English as-a-second-language student. There is no pressure; nor is there an expectation of immediate native-English fluency. From hearing and reading English, ESL students become familiar with the sound of English discourse in contexts that become increasingly more meaningful.

Having dispelled any doubts about whether Juan will learn the language well enough to handle *Charlotte's Web*, Gonzales points out that the other kids in the classroom are actually **responsible** for Juan's learning.

> In collaborative learning, students all share responsibility for performance. Each student is responsible for the learning of others. Students are expected to help and encourage others so that all can succeed. There is positive interdependence with division of labor. Perhaps joint rewards are given.

Nothing in the California education code suggests that the kids actually have this responsibility. (And I don't think the teachers unions would take too kindly to it.) But according to Gonzales' conception of cooperative learning, if Juan and the others don't learn, the teacher is not to blame. Everybody shares the blame, because everybody shares the responsibility.

> Because the teacher may have difficulty meeting the content needs of various students, the whole class is involved in the process of ensuring that all students have sufficient background to make sense of the reading selection or become prepared to respond to a writing assignment. Likewise, everyone in the class is active in negotiating the understanding derived from lessons. Finally, all students share the relationships between the literature they are reading and writing and their own lives.

Juan's parents may not understand that their boy's educational future rests in the hands of classmates and the happy circumstances that permit them to instruct Juan.

Ultimately, however, Juan sits alone and must take responsibility for his failure. After all, everyone is active in negotiating the understanding derived from the lesson. This understanding is an individual one (unless Gonzales' classroom somehow implants a "group mind" into the cooperative little learners). Also, the sharing of relationships between the literature students read and write and their "own lives" is an individual pursuit. Since Juan is unable to perform on either of these "negotiations," he's apparently the only one to blame.

The teacher can't be held responsible because she "may have difficulty meeting the content needs of various students." The class can't be held responsible for Juan's poor preparation because they are not actually "responsible" for his preparation, and because they probably have serious problems of their own. After all, they're in a classroom with no presumed sequence for the things the teacher will spring on them.

Gonzales has a final solution for kids like Juan, but it raises some questions about "access to the core curriculum for all students."

> Whenever limited-English-proficient students do not understand a lesson, the teacher and other students vary the way it is presented. When written language is not understood, then it is helped by discussions. When discussions are not comprehended, visuals accompany the lesson. When visuals don't communicate the message, dramatizations are employed.

Chapter 5: The Supporting Cast

So the bottom line seems to be that Juan has access to pictures and a puppet show, accompanied by babbling that he doesn't understand, but that is supposed to teach him about Manifest Destiny. Somehow, this image seems to be in conflict with the title of Gonzales' article: "Equity and Access in a Language Arts Program for All Students."

I know nothing of Gonzales' background (except that he has obviously never taught kids effectively). His conclusions about equity would be understandable if he'd worked on school bussing before writing his article. Kids who have a seat on the bus have access to the bus. "Hey mom, I got me a seat in the front row." Through extrapolation it follows that kids who have a seat in the classroom have access to the "lesson" delivered to the class. If the teacher presents the core curriculum to the class, the kids who are sitting must have access to the core curriculum. And if access implies equity, Juan is all set. His seat in the classroom is just as good as Jennifer's.

Gonzales' solutions raise an interesting question: Since the kids in Juan's classroom represent such a wide spread in performance, and since there is no presumed sequence for teaching skills, why not go all the way and eliminate the niggling requirement that all the kids are the same age? If neither skill level nor the material presented constrains, the ultimate solution for California should be a building that has one room and kids from possibly 4 to 16 years old, all engaged by a single teacher (and the cooperative efforts of the students in the class).

CHAPTER 6
ACADEMIC CHILD ABUSE

The logic of the NCTE and California decision makers are not isolated examples. We see the same type of logic in other professional groups, such as the National Council of Teachers of Mathematics, and in most school districts. Although the organizations and districts are perfectly naive about how to achieve the outcomes their scenarios promise, they proceed with undiluted confidence.

Their outrageous stance springs from the sorting-machine philosophy that has characterized U.S. public education from its inception. The philosophy is based on the notion that the schools do what the schools choose to do, and if kids fail, it's their own fault. Historically, this philosophy was functional. It served to sort out kids so that only a small percentage went to college and beyond. These kids were the survivors, the ones who had the grit, the smarts, and sand necessary to meet the Herculean challenges the school masters presented. The overwhelming number failed and landed in the large agricultural and unskilled labor force, or in the then-small white-collar class.

Over the years, reforms have superficially changed the schools, but the sorting machine has survived and remains the central reason both for the discrepancy between practice and the rhetoric of educators and for the school's policy of failing a very high percentage of the school population. During the time in which Horace Mann was fashioning reform and promoting school success, over half the kids in all the large-city systems for which there was data, failed. The same ratio obtains today.

The 20th Century has seen the first kindergartens, miscellaneous curriculum reforms, and possibly the biggest change, attempts to integrate and deal with disadvantaged kids. The sorting machine has accommodated all these changes. I recall that at the time bussing and integration were planned, I had a disagreement with a respected colleague. His idea was that the integration would improve teaching because it would force teachers to learn better teaching techniques for

59

working with the disadvantaged kids. My position was that the only possible thing that could happen was a lowering of standards, because the teachers in middle-class schools had never tried to work with kids as low as the average disadvantaged kid, and the teachers wouldn't learn anything from the experience. If they were to pass these kids from grade to grade, they'd have to lower their standards.

They did. It was predictable because the only philosophy the schools ever had was a sorting-machine philosophy. Accordingly, kids were at fault for any failures. Administrators were confronted with failures that society wasn't ready to accept as failures; therefore, the schools had to pretend that failure wasn't failure.

The history of educational rhetoric has always been rosy, liberal, and in stark contrast to the sorting-machine realities of the schools. Consider the introduction of "look-say," or sight basal reading programs. Why did they come into such favor in the schools? Largely because John Dewey advocated them. He needed grist for his learning-by-doing mill but all he had were cooking classes, and he needed some academic skill in which kids could "do it" immediately. Enter look-say reading, which does not first prepare the kids to read but presents reading immediately, on day one. This approach fit in with Dewey's philosophy, and major school districts installed it. The installation was a sorting-machine decision. The administrators had no evidence that it worked well; there was, at the time, strong evidence to suggest that it didn't. However, matters of effectiveness and efficiency are fundamentally incompatible with the sorting-machine orientation.

The rhetoric and theories of educators have been a very dependable handmaiden of school failures. Possibly the best way to view popular educational ideas is in terms of supply and demand. When schools fail, they need a rationale or theory that will somehow displace the issue and make the failures trivial compared to some unnoticed success. So, educators search the market place of philosophies or viewpoints to find those that present (in the educator's estimation) credible arguments. The failure of the new math demanded a philosophy. The philosophical market place provided one—humanism. Human values were important; math and science were the product of a linear, product-oriented, mechanistic view of the world. Bad. When blacks failed, educators turned to "sociolinguists," who demonstrated that the pen is mightier than the facts by "proving" that black English was capable of all the subtleties of standard English, and therefore, that ghetto blacks were as smart as middle-class whites. Naturally, the "sociolinguists" didn't deal with the issue of performance—how much a particular black first grader knows about black English, or standard English. (There were some studies that showed the deficiencies of ghetto blacks in black English, but these studies were largely ignored.)

A standby of the "modern" educator is "developmental theory" which is largely irrelevant to any type of instructional application. The educator's love for developmental theories is greatly suspect for another reason: developmental theories feed the sorting machine by describing "stages" and typical behaviors of kids at different "stages." While some of the more basic facts of development are as obvious as the fact that preschoolers are smaller than fifth graders, I know of no application of developmental theory to instruction that has provided an exemplary practice.

Schools have three reasons for using developmental philosophies. The first is that they sound very humane and thoughtful. That's important. The second is that they permit the school to transfer failure from the real cause—poor teaching—to the kids. Third, educators can use developmental philosophies to redefine "failure." When an educator asserts, "Children learn naturally through play, and they should not be stifled by an archaic work ethic that runs counter to facts of child development," people tend to believe that these words are based on some evidence. When a parent is later told by a school administrator or a school psychologist, "Billy is not developmentally ready to handle reading," the parent often has no recourse but to accept this seemingly thoughtful diagnosis.

The logic of "readiness" is not very compelling. A kid fails, and it becomes an axiom that the kid was not ready. It's never the case that the teacher was not ready to teach Billy. It's always the case that Billy was not ready to learn.

Another handy philosophy is the one that elevated Kenneth Goodman to a position of respectability in educational circles—his "miscue analysis." Here's the setting: All major school districts were using look-say basal reading programs. These programs are notorious for inducing word guessing. The reason they promote this behavior is that they have been fashioned from the same logic that drives "whole-language," the idea that reading for "meaning" is both the name of the game and the process that should be taught from the beginning of grade one. The look-say basals confuse kids in a lot of ways. One is by not showing them that a particular letter like **b** must be oriented in a particular way or it's not **b**, but becomes **d**, **p**, or **q** (which is unique to the kid's experience, because any object—a box, a cup, or a refrigerator—keeps the same object name even if it's upside down). But possibly an even greater source of confusion is that these programs **imply** that you must understand what you'll read before you read it. This notion is prompted by first-grade procedures that have the teacher first talk about the characters in the book and what they are doing **before** the kids read the words. This process is backwards. The kids should read first because the words should be the source of meaning that determines what the picture would show. The problem is confounded by very predictable texts, in which the kids can call out the correct words, not by actually reading them, but by guessing. "Tom went to the store. Sally went ____." Finally, the approach actually encourages kids to **guess**. Teachers are told to prompt kids to look at the "general shape" of the word, or "figure out the word from context." "Well, what do you think that word is?" (Good readers don't read this way. Studies show that even when readers read very fast, they perceive individual letters and precise sequences of letters.)

The product of the look-say basal is the typical problem reader—who reads in synonyms, guesses at words that are in sentences, and tries to figure out words by their beginning letter or shape. In other words, the corrective reader does all the silly things teachers told him to do. Consider the terribly involved process you'd have to go through to read like a corrective reader. You'd have to be able to recognize a word like **small**, and then you'd have to search for some linguistic counterpart that matched your knowledge of the meaning, **small**, not of the precise appearance of **small**. So, in searching for a word that has the right meaning, you might come out with "little," which some teachers do not accept as "correct."

Once, when we were working on the development of a corrective reading program, a kid let me in on the incredible mental gyrations he went through while reading. The kids (all in junior high) had been taught basic rules about "sounding out" words. One kid was reading a sentence aloud and made a "synonym" mistake. The teacher said, "Sound it out."

The kid looked at her and said, "Tell me the word and I'll sound it out."

At first I thought the kid was being a smart aleck, but then I realized, he said it all. "I must know the meaning before I can pronounce the word."

No rational argument can be provided to justify misteaching kids, a practice that "erodes" kids' confidence—for very good reasons. These kids know they are poor readers and they don't like it. But the educators who used look-say or whole language were not ready to accept the fact that they caused this kind of failure. How did they solve their problem? They went to the market-place of philosophies to find something that could disguise this failure. And there it was: Goodman's miscue analysis. It reassured teachers that kids who guess are performing perfectly marvelous "linguistic feats." Reading "the" for **a**, or "the" for **this**, were not considered mistakes but evidence that kids understood what they read. There were unanswered questions about substitutions like "what" for **that** or "did" for **didn't**. But Goodman's "theory" was apparently good enough for decision makers. Goodman became president of the International Reading Association. Teachers applauded his noble insights without ever observing the shadow of the sorting machine.

If the educational decision makers were consistent with their rhetoric, they would have to abandon all aspects of sorting-machine philosophies and all sorting-machine practices. Accountability and sorting machines are incompatible; intelligent instruction and sorting-machines are in compatible. Sorting-machine philosophy **considers the decision makers first**. The philosophy that considers kids first goes something like this: **If the kid hasn't learned, the teacher hasn't taught**.

This is not a slogan. It's a way of life. It means that kids are capable of learning if we show our empathy not through cheap rhetoric, but through deeds. We look at things from the kids' perspective. We carefully assess what the kids know, always with the understanding that kids are the final authority and that their misconceptions are reasonable responses to what they have been told and shown. We start out where the kids are and where they can succeed—even if the starting point is pretty far from where we'd like it to be. Then we teach carefully, using the kids' performance as our only reference point for measuring our success. If that kid fails, we failed, and we'll have to go back to the drawing board and learn more about doing a better job. We don't use a floating standard. With a floating standard, we could fail to teach half the kids in a classroom. At the end of the year, we could proudly point to the kids who learned and say, "I taught them." When asked about the other kids, we would say, "Oh, they were not ready to learn." We must play the game straight. If we take credit for the kids who succeed, we must take credit for those who failed.

Interestingly enough, the traditional educational establishment is offended by the premise: If the learner hasn't learned, the teacher hasn't taught. An excellent trainer in New York City, Janie Feinberg, operates a learning center, primarily for school failures. She does a very good job. Several years ago, she distributed T-shirts. On the front was written, "Center for Direct Instruction" and in larger print, the motto: "If the learner hasn't learned, the teacher hasn't taught." She got lots of calls and letters complaining about this hideous motto—even from teacher union officials. At first blush, the motto may seem to imply that it blames teachers, but the fact is that kids who haven't learned haven't been taught. If we start arguing this point, suggesting possibly that "learning is an individual pursuit that can't be taught," we're actually talking in sorting-machine language. The schools are our agency for teaching, not for making excuses or redefining success and failure.

For schools to adopt the empathic premise about learning, they'd have to learn about instruction and make instructional details and kid performance the central foci of their operation. That implies an administration, or at least a segment of it, that is knowledgeable about instruction. Districts do not have such a segment. Although school districts typically have enormous administrations (more administrators in New York state than in all of Western Europe) instructional knowledge is neither a criterion nor a function of this machine. Certainly, people within places like New York state have titles that suggest instructional knowledge—reading supervisors, elementary supervisors, trainers, and so forth. But if we were to put them in a classroom and have them deal with instructional problems—diagnosing them, providing a remedy that works now, and possibly predicting precisely what the kids will do when the remedy is introduced—we would probably discover that no more than five percent of them would pass the test. Most would be a sham in the classroom and would actually teach no better than the average teacher. They became supervisors, in the overwhelming number of cases, not by being star teachers, but for other political considerations (often because of their philosophical outlook). There are exceptions, and I apologize to those people, but they know how lonely it is to understand instruction and have to try to deal with an administration that is not only naive, but doesn't really care (despite the rhetoric).

If I'm overstating the case, we should be able to identify aspects of school instructional practices that violate the sorting-machine rule. Let's see.

The teacher is "master" of the classroom and, in the typical school system, receives no training. That's the sorting-machine, not empathy for kids. Studies show that teachers do better when supervised regularly and that teachers are not good at identifying solutions to teaching problems. To let teachers alone in the classroom is to acknowledge that the kids are not the most important aspect of the schools. To let kids fail throughout the year and do nothing about it is perfectly irresponsible. Schools do it regularly. One point for the sorting machine.

We've seen programs that have never been tried out with kids (à la new wave of programs adopted in California) find their way quickly into the schools. That's wholesale experimentation with kids as guinea pigs. Two points for the sorting machine.

The latest trend in schools is to encourage parents to work with kids on academics. For instance, the California *Framework* presents a list of "effective and ineffective" features for language-arts programs.

Included in the list of effective features is: "A home environment where parents model effective listening, speaking, reading, and writing and offer appropriate help with their children's homework." The ineffective counterpart: "A home environment where parents play a passive role as their children are learning the language arts."

In case you don't recognize blatant discrimination, this "effective feature" is an example. A poverty kid probably has a "passive home environment." Juan's parents may not model effective speaking. The kid fails, and the schools blame not only the kid, but also the parents. Similarly, a middle-class kid fails. The system stands in judgment of the parents, suggesting that they didn't do their job. The school implies that it did its job by providing the experiment, the unsupervised teachers, and an extensive administration. All the parents had to do was teach the kid. One more point for the sorting machine.

What about standardized testing? Although it is currently under attack by the new wave of "reform," it is based on the sorting-machine. Achievement tests do not test program content (things that the kids have been taught in the program they studied), but they test a broad range of items to determine something about the kid's "aptitude." Test failure, as the schools interpret it, does not suggest failures of teachers, but kid failure. One more point for the sorting machine.

If there's any doubt that tests are interpreted in this manner, consider the basic diagnostic scheme used in the schools. A kid has trouble. A school psychologist sometimes gives the kid "tests" and determines the problem. If the system were accountable and based on the notion that if the kid fails the teaching failed, a lot of diagnoses would hold that the kid has performance problems but the **cause** of the problem is the teaching. If the sorting machine is in place, all diagnoses would take the form that the kid has learning problems, **and** the kid is the cause of the problem. (There's something wrong with the kid.)

In 1978, an investigator named Coles reviewed research on "learning disabilities." In the studies he reviewed (about 1000) not **one** considered the relationship between instruction or other school factors and the learning disability. Galen Alessi wrote an article in 1988 in which he diagnosed diagnosis. He asked 50 school psychologists to indicate how many cases they referred during the year. The average was about

100 per psychologist; so the group provided information on about 5000 kids. Alessi next tried to determine the different **causes** of the kid's learning problems. How many of the kids had the learning problem because of inappropriate curriculum? How many had learning problems because of poor teaching, or because of school administration problems? How many kids had problems because of home problems, or because there was some defect in the kid?

The percentages came out something like this:

- The curriculum caused 0% of the referred problems;
- The teaching practices caused 0% of the referred problems;
- The school administration caused 0% of the referred problems;
- The home environment caused 10-20% of the referred problems;
- The child caused 100% of the referred problems.

The results tend to leave little doubt about whether the school psychologists work for the schools or the children. It further leaves no doubt that the sorting machine is alive and well. Consider the presumed infallibility of the schools suggested by this outcome. Not one of 5000 failures is presumed to be caused by school practices. Two points and one bonus point for the sorting machine.

The final aspect of the sorting-machine philosophy is the unbounded arrogance of school administrators and decision makers. They have very strong opinions about how children should be taught and the general methods that should be used. Yet, they have precisely no experience in producing outstanding teaching outcomes. If we were to permit people to have opinions to the degree that they had first-hand actual experience with exemplary practices, most administrators would be mute when it came to any detail of instruction. The fact that they have no personal basis for their opinions, but are extremely vocal about what should be done, raises a question about the basis for this arrogance. It's not observed in medicine, or any other field. You don't find people who have never learned basic surgical techniques posing as experts on surgery. You wouldn't even find a person who knew nothing about automobile engines proclaiming to be an expert mechanic.

Chapter 6: Academic Child Abuse

The arrogance of many administrators is not apparent in their personality. They may appear thoughtful, concerned, and open to suggestions. Their arrogance is in their decisions and their actions. Their actions reflect a fundamental lack of important values. Galen Alessi alluded to the problem with school psychologists: "Mere logic and research data will not change the role of school psychology, because the problem is not one of science but of values."

Not long ago, an ex-trainer in our Follow Through project reminded me of a lesson she learned about these values. She had been a student teacher at the time, working in a classroom of blue-collar kids. During a period scheduled for reading, she was engaging the kids in a pointless discussion. I told her trainer to take over the group she was working with, while I took her aside. I told her something to the effect: "When you work with those kids, they are your kids, and whatever you do must be what you would want to happen if you were their parent. The parents can't teach them effectively. That's why you're here. You remember that, and if you can't, don't try to be a teacher."

After she recalled this incident, she observed, "That's what's lacking in the schools. There's all this talk about doing wonderful things for the kids, but when you look at what actually happens, that basic moral core is missing."

I agree. But things will change in education only when the field of education adopts a new cornerstone philosophy that permits accountability and a moral stand about what the teacher or administrator must do. Reforms are a paradox within the current system because, while rhetoric refers to avant-garde approaches, practices belch from the Model T sorting machine. The basic philosophy of the sorting machine operates on every aspect of current schools. Changing parts of this system won't work. The sorting machine must be scrapped, from the conceptual level, and replaced with a philosophy of empathy for kids.

A recently formed group, The International Institute of Advocacy for School Children (I'ASC), refers to the sorting-machine practices of the schools as **academic child abuse**. This form of abuse does not have the legal status of ordinary "child abuse," but it is just as painful to the kids and their families. I'ASC defines **academic child abuse** as "the use of practices that cause unnecessary failure of foundation skills." The definition is limited to groups of children, not to individuals. The judgment about unnecessary failure is based on a comparison of "what is judged possible with the same school budget and the same setting, but with different practices."

Schools are guilty of much academic child abuse because they don't approach the performance standards that could be met if they used enlightened practices. This school failure is not the failure of kids, and often not the failure of teachers. It's the failure of a sick system that places more value on the whims of adults than on the obvious needs of children.

CHAPTER 7
LET'S GO TO COURT

In August, 1988 when I wrote my first letter to the members of the California State Board, the Curriculum Commission had already sent the Board its "Recommendations of Instructional Materials for Adoption; 1988 English-Language Arts." *Reading Mastery* appeared on the list of programs not recommended for approval.

The Commission's report presented a glib summary of research that shaped the adoption strategies. The text reads like other state propaganda about education:

> Excessive use of skill exercises deprives learners of the sound and sense of the language they need in order to construct their own understandings of how language works. Even those children who cannot read or write before first grade, naturally learn skills within the context of getting and making meaning.

Notice that the Commission solves the reading problem by making reading easy, natural. "Even those children who cannot read or write before first grade…" Are we to believe the number is small? How then is it possible for so many California fourth graders to function on the first-grade level?

My first letter to the Board members complained about the Commission's recommendations and the other "irregularities" in the adoption process. The president of the Board, Dr. Francis Laufenberg, responded with a letter that seemed to invite me to present at a public hearing. Here's part of Laufenberg's letter:

> As you are no doubt aware, the Commission's recommendations will be formally presented to the Board at its September meeting. At that time, an opportunity will be provided for all interested and concerned parties to make their comments, opinions, and positions known. I realize that attending this meeting would represent both a hardship and an expense for you, but I urge you to do so if at all possible in order to present

and discuss your thoughts orally. I do not wish to make any prejudicial statements (one way or the other) concerning your comments, but it is obvious that your opinions are strong and that you are knowledgeable in the subject matter area under consideration. The Board is composed of the lay public (though some of us have had past experience as public school teachers and administrators), and I can assure that we will give full and fair consideration **both** to the Commission's recommendations and to **all** the concerns which may be voiced regarding those recommendations.

What image does that imply—presenting, discussing, full and fair consideration?

More than 25 presenters were apparently prepared to "present and discuss their thoughts orally" at the hearing. I had written a paper that would probably take 10 minutes to present. The meeting began with the announcement that each presenter would be limited to two minutes. Several other agenda items preceded the Commission's recommendations, but finally, the Commission's hearing began with a two-person, dramatic reading of the Commission's recommendations—from the beginning:

> Performer 1: There were no drum rolls! There were no clarion calls! Yet, during the week of June 20-24, 1988, there was a calm assurance by Instructional Materials Evaluation Panel members that California's English-Language arts adoption for kindergarten through grade eight was carrying on the legacy of the "quiet revolution" begun in 1983. As a result, teachers will have better instructional materials to help students improve their language arts through their experiences with literature.

> Performer 2: While this process has indicated that literature is no longer an endangered species in our classrooms, we still need to be wary about how literature is used in language programs...

The room was packed; the day hot; the lobbyist anxious to get on with it. The reading continued for possibly five minutes before a Board member pulled the plug on it.

The Board had two featured speakers (who were not restricted to two minutes). The first was Richard Anderson, Director of the Center for the Study of Reading.

Anderson's talk explained that the adoption process may have been colored by prejudices. He noted that "the most zealous proponents of "whole language" are as noteworthy for what they are against as what they are for. They absolutely proscribe teaching skills in isolation, which in their minds rules out traditional, systematic approaches to phonics." Anderson observed that the research supports phonics instruction in the beginning grades but that there was a pattern among the rejected programs: "All of them have a reputation for intensive phonics instruction in the lower grades."

The biggest problem, according to Anderson, is that the format of the adoption process used by California can't work. "The adoption recommendation before you is flawed—not simply because of quirks this year—but because of inherent shortcomings in the statewide adoption process." Anderson listed flaws in the system: under preparation of the reviewers, inadequate time for a thorough review, and a system subject to abuses, including fraud and bribery. "It is vulnerable to ideological fashion. It is expensive and time consuming. Scholars who have studied the statewide adoption process concur that it is an unwise intrusion in the market place. Ideally, there would be no state adoption at all."

Anderson's recommendations: "First, this year accept all of the reading programs submitted. Second, henceforth, abandon statewide textbook adoption."

The matter of doing away with statewide adoptions is not that simple for California. The adoption duties of the Board are specified by the California Constitution. To do away with them would require a constitutional amendment (which wouldn't be a bad idea).

The other presenter allotted more than two minutes was Assembly person Maxine Waters, who spoke on behalf of Foundations for

Learning in Los Angeles. Maxine's plea was that the disadvantaged kids in the Foundations' program were far removed from literature in the beginning grades and needed an approach that could communicate on their level. The Board and audience applauded her presentation; yet, she was saying in effect that the search for "meaning" that was appropriate for her kids did not involve the mandate of California's new approach, "literature."

When it was my turn to give my rendition of the two-minute drill, I did what I could to explain why *Reading Mastery* should be adopted. I raised some questions about the Board's policies and was asking the Board questions when my two minutes ran out: "What are you going to do when your plan fails? What are you going to say to the school districts that have used *Reading Mastery* with success and now may have to drop the program because of pressure from the *Framework*?"

Ms. Hom, the chairperson, pounded her gavel with great conviction, and my time to present and discuss my thoughts orally was over.

Following the public hearing, the Board "disapproved" *Reading Mastery*. Afterwards, Laufenberg told Steve Osborn, the only other presenter at the public hearing to speak on behalf of *Reading Mastery*, that the Board's decision might have been different if more people had spoken for *Reading Mastery*. I have a lot of trouble with this logic. If there is one area in which numbers will not correspond to truth, it's education. A relatively obvious rule of thumb is that the opinions of the majority are those that drive the typical instructional approaches used in schools. These approaches fail. It would seem to follow that the opinions of the majority are therefore worthless for determining what works.

In some ways, I can sympathize with Board members. They were subjected to a bombardment of the same tired themes about the search for meaning and literature—a siege of rhetoric from many educators, the Department of Education, and the Curriculum Commission. Being "lay people," they may have assumed that if so many professionals agree, they must be right. After all, they are the professionals. On the other hand, I can't sympathize with the Board members. I sent the Board a lot of information that could be checked out if (a) one is capable of reading, and (b) one chooses to check the validity of the assertions that I made.

One article that I sent the Board was written by Cathy Watkins. Its title says it all: "Project Follow Through: A Story of The Identification and Neglect of Effective Instruction." As Watkins put it, "The educational establishment's vested interests have effectively prevented the largest experiment in the history of instructional methods (costing almost one billion dollars) from having the impact on daily classroom practices that its results clearly warranted."

Assuming that the Board members know how to read and were awake when Anderson and Waters explained obvious problems with the adoption process, we are left with only a couple of possible explanations for the Board's reasoning. The most obvious is that the Board members don't really think that instructional programs make a difference. Possibly, they believe that all teachers need to succeed is lots of good will and slogans about the search for meaning. Possibly, they, like others on the periphery of instruction, really believe that something is a reform if Bill Honig says it's a reform. During the adoption process, a headline from the *San Diego Tribune* asserted that, "War on 'Dumb' Textbooks Draws Publisher Protests." According to Honig, the protests were merely grumblings of publishers whose products didn't "measure up."

I didn't like what was happening in California. *Reading Mastery* had been framed as something that you wouldn't want to see in the classroom, something that was dumb. Districts that had been using *Reading Mastery*—some with extremely good results—were bailing out and jumping on the whole-language bandwagon, and their kids were going down the tubes.

Only one route seemed capable of stopping the state from further abuses of power, and that was the legal route. The route has many blockades because so long as the Board, Honig, and the Department operate in the "public interest," they are all but immune from lawsuits. California, however, went too far. The Board obviously works for Honig (instead of directing him) and the Board has a history of ignoring statutes and rubber stamping "guidelines" that are treated as formal regulations.

Chapter 7: Let's Go to Court

So on June 21, 1989, I brought suit against the State Board of Education, the Department of Education, and the Curriculum Commission. The issues were based on administrative law and dealt with the process (or lack of it) that the Board and Department of Education used to make decisions. The central question was whether the Board, Honig et al., could simply make up rules as they went along, regardless of the impact they would have on kids and parents. The state did not follow procedures specified in the Administrative Procedure Act (APA) which provides more protection for people affected by administrative decisions.

The suit called for declaring that the standards, criteria, evaluation worksheets, and other material designed by the state to adopt reading material were illegal. The suit also called for commanding the Board and Department of Education to follow APA procedures when establishing new standards, criteria, and evaluation worksheets.

Unfortunately, in California this type of suit (petition for writ of mandate and declaratory relief) does not involve a trial with witnesses and courtroom drama. I would have loved for people like Gonzales to take the stand, where they would have had to respond to very pointed questions. In California, the petition is handled much like an appeal. The petitioner (that's me) submits a preliminary statement—a lengthy brief. If the court judges that there's a basis for a suit, the petitioner receives a trial date and presents more documents—starting with a memorandum of points and authorities. The state responds with a rebuttal. Finally, the petitioner responds to the rebuttal. The briefs go to a judge before the trial. The judge studies the arguments. The trial lasts less than two hours and consists of short oral arguments, questions from the judge, and a decision, usually on the spot.

My attorney was Jay-Allen Eisen, a very talented Sacramento lawyer who had an impressive record in thrashing agencies. He is an expert on APA. In his initial petition, he laid out the argument that the criteria, policies, procedures, manuals, and the like for adopting instructional material should be null and void because they hadn't been promulgated in accordance with the APA. The argument documents that the Board is not uniquely exempt from APA, that the Board had not followed the procedural requirements of the APA, and that the criteria, worksheets and other material are regulations and are therefore subject to APA rule making. A second argument pointed out that the Board's policies conflict with governing statutes.

Although the APA practices don't guarantee competence by an agency, they present many more safeguards than those provided by procedures California used. First, under APA, the agency would have to, "Make available to interested members of the public a statement containing the agency's rationale for the proposed policy and identification of each technical, theoretical, and empirical study, report or similar document on which the agency may be relying."

Furthermore, the agency would have to "base its final action on the evidence and argument contained in the official administrative record," and "justify its final regulations in light of comments from interested members of the public, or justify the rejection of those arguments."

The agency, in other words, would have to respond to criticisms or data that contradicts its "theories" or "research." The agency would not be permitted the luxury of staging public hearings that are complete farces designed only to give the appearance that the Board is "fair." Finally, the agency would have to, "Obtain approval of the Office of Administrative Law, which, among other things, determines the necessity and authority for the regulations."

The requirement of getting approval from the Office of Administrative Law is probably a very good one because lawyers are far more rational than educators. They understand the difference between facts and opinion, theory and data.

The State's answer to the petition seemed incredible. It argued that the Board had a "self-executing" authority to do basically whatever it chose to do in adopting textbooks and that the Board's actions were not subject to review by the **legislature** or the Office of Administrative Law. The State's argument is based on the California Constitution and three earlier decisions. Section 7.5 of the State Constitution provides: "The State Board of Education shall adopt textbooks for use in grades one through eight throughout the State, to be furnished without cost as provided by statute."

Chapter 7: Let's Go to Court

The State interpreted this duty and three cases as evidence that, "Respondent would be within its authority to ignore all of part 33 [of the California Education Code] which deals with the evaluation and selection of textbooks." In other words, the Board could ignore all **statutes** concerning adoption.

While this argument may seem extreme, the Board was probably not the best client a lawyer ever had. The Board had largely ignored statutes that referred to maximizing pupil performance and "learner verification" (documentation that instructional programs work well).

These statutes were adopted by the legislature in 1976. The main statute (Section 60226) provides that "publishers and manufacturers shall, in accordance with rules and regulations adopted by the State Board, develop plans to improve the quality and reliability of instructional materials through learner verification."

Learner verification is defined as "continuous and thorough evaluation of instructional materials for their effectiveness with pupils." The legislation seems perfectly reasonable. By working out plans for the "thorough evaluation of the materials," the Board would overcome one of the problems with the adoption process (the superficial nature of the evaluation). It would also permit the state to secure first-hand data on how well different programs work with kids and teachers and how much training is required for teachers to implement them appropriately. The state would not only become more knowledgeable about the facts of instruction. It would serve as an advocate for the consumers of instruction—teachers, kids, and parents.

The 1988 adoption presented publishers with cryptic requirements related to "learner-verification data." Publishers were to provide a "description of the field-testing process" for the submitted material and "an explanation of how materials are to be developed, improved, and/or maintained, on the basis of the field-testing data collected." The requirement for submitting this information is strange because the information wasn't to be used. Following the specifications of the information publishers were to submit on learner verification, the instructions declared:

"This additional information is not to be considered as part of the criteria for recommending materials to the State Board of Education in the 1988 English/Language Arts adoption."

The State's legal brief had a quaint way of explaining the Board's "use" of field-test information. "Respondent decided not to consider such information to be the equivalent of its substantive adoption criteria." The word **substantive** in this sentence should be bronzed. Awarding the learner verification no consideration whatsoever is indeed not considering it to be the equivalent of the state's "criteria."

The State also argued that the Board had formally adopted guidelines for learner verification on June 10, 1988. If adoption occurred on this date, it occurred **after** the 1988 adoption of instructional programs had been completed.

The trial was scheduled on Friday the 13th, a poor omen for one of the parties involved. The judge did not make a decision on the spot, or even within a few days. The decision came on November 14th, 1989. I won. The Superior Court decision, rendered by James Long, compelled the State Board to adopt, in compliance with APA, "any policies and procedures, standards or evaluation instruments which are used to carry out the Board's responsibility to adopt textbooks and instructional material."

The court also compelled the State Board to adopt "regulations directing publishers in the development of learner verification plans for instructions submitted for adoption by the Board." Finally, the decision compelled the Department of Education, the Board, and the Curriculum Commission "to refrain during the process of adopting textbooks and instructional materials from using or relying on any policies and procedures, standards or evaluation instruments which have not been adopted in compliance with the procedural requirements of the Administrative Procedure Act..."

My legal victory over California may have been a hollow one, and the outcome of the suit may do nothing more than make the Board jump through a few more hoops before engaging in academic child abuse. Barbara Bateman, a professor of Special Education who also has a degree in law, reviewed the case for the Reading Reform Foundation, and her conclusions were reserved (because she knows how pathetic the law is as an advocate for kids in instructional matters). She observed:

> The APA requires that policies and procedures be adopted in a more public, open way and that there be a reasonable basis for agency decisions. However, the legal meaning of reasonable is merely that it **not** be totally arbitrary, capricious or unreasonable. If it has any basis it will be upheld. Thus, even if the Board were to follow APA slavishly, it would not necessarily mean better adoptions would result. It would mean the process would be more visible and subject to scrutiny.
>
> Would districts pay attention to publishers' data on program effectiveness? Would the Board adopt rules for publishers which would require the publishers to examine how well children learned to read? Or might the rules instead allow data on how much teachers enjoy teaching from the material, or on how the children "feel" about language arts? The strength of the forces in education that oppose data-based decision making should not be underestimated.
>
> The final chapter of this lawsuit remains to be written in the adoption process itself. There may or may not be intermediate chapters in the courts. At a minimum, the California State Board of Education has learned that Siegfried Engelmann not only designs the most effective instructional programs ever seen, but he can also design an effective lawsuit.

As Bateman's conclusion indicates, there is no guard against incompetence in education; however, if the process is visible, possibly people who know something about instruction will step forward, if not to tell what they know, at least to explain why the establishment doesn't understand what it's saying. Bateman's conclusion also suggests that the game is to do things that work for kids. I personally don't care about whether anybody uses the programs I've developed. That's not the issue. The issue is: Are all the kids being taught and taught effectively? If they are, whatever the school district is doing must be quite adequate. But if the district is plagued with failure—as most California districts are—intelligent changes must follow.

The response of the legislators and the major newspapers in the state to the suit was curious. Actually, it was non-existent. Eisen sent releases to every major newspaper in the state. Not one (to the best of my knowledge) printed a single word about the suit. Here the state was, without any legally adopted guidelines or criteria for reading-language arts programs. The State Department of Education could not enforce or use any of this material to interact with the districts in matters of adoption. The Board was shown to be illegal and largely irresponsible for not complying with governing statutes; however, not one word about the suit. Key state legislators received letters explaining the suit and its implication for school districts. Not one legislator responded. About the only publicity the suit received was from a national publication, *Education Week*. On November 29, 1989, it carried an article that never really questioned whether the California reforms were actually reforms, or were what the suit suggested—illegal activities. The article stated that the California guidelines had been judged illegal and observed, "Over the past few years, the Board has used such guidelines in widely publicized efforts to implement substantial curricular reforms. Led by Superintendent of Public Instruction, Bill Honig, California officials have made their textbook adoption process the focal point for implementing curricular change."

They certainly have. Honig's name appears on the front page of each of California's reform documents.

In 1989, the Little Hoover Commission petitioned the State's Attorney to investigate Honig because of his obvious arrogation of authority over the Board and his practice of issuing guidelines instead of formally adopted regulations.

In 1990, I wrote an article for the California *Journal for Supervision and Curriculum Improvement*, which went to every principal in the state. The article told about the suit, pointed out the problems of legality in the schools, and suggested the moral problem facing administrators.

"The schools in your district may have installed whole-language reading on the assumption not merely that it was innovative, but that it would work." The test of how well it is working is in the classroom. If there's a lot of failure, there are problems. "These children can be taught with effective methods, but methods that have been demonstrated to be effective bear little resemblance to those currently used in California."

How many calls or letters did the editor of the *Journal* receive about this article? None. In the same issue was a pathetic "rejoinder" from a California bureaucrat, Glen Thomas. Possibly, California administrators understand that when the Department of Education presents a "rejoinder," all moral issues are officially decided. The sorting machine has spoken.

In a world more just than ours, however, Honig and Gonzales would team-teach a fourth grade—50 kids who exhibit the full range of student variation (or non-variation, as the case may be). Their performance would be videotaped, and then at the end of the year, when Honig and Gonzales couldn't hide in the comforting prose of "equity" or lie about their obvious failure, we'd gather great insight into how something billed as "reform" can actually be very effective discrimination and academic child abuse.

CHAPTER 8

EFFECTIVE TEACHING

The central cause of all failure in school is the teaching. When the teaching fails, the kids fail. This fact seems obvious enough; however, the solution of correcting the teaching is more elusive to reformers. They tend to recommend "upgrading" the teaching in some unspecified way. They sometimes turn to "motivational magic" and assume that if the teacher had more autonomy, more incentives, higher pay, the teaching would improve.

Possibly, these remedies will produce some improvement. In most cases, however, the cause of kid failure is the curriculum. The curriculum, after all, provides the specifications of what the teacher is to teach and therefore what the kids are to learn. If the curriculum is lumpy, the teaching suffers.

Amy is an example of a teacher who is victimized by her instructional material. She teaches fourth grade, using one of those traditional basal programs that presents a succession of topics like "main idea," "fact versus opinion," and "cause and effect." Amy doesn't know that the programs are causing a lot of the effects she observes in her kids, but she does know that the kids have a lot of trouble.

Like most teachers, Amy is not an ace diagnostician of student problems or an instructional designer. The closest Amy ever came to experiencing instructional design in college, occurred in her senior year of college when she made a creative bulletin board. When her kids don't learn, Amy doesn't know exactly what to do, except to keep trying. Like the other day, when she tried to teach main idea. The first three passages the kids read from their basal presented the main idea in the first sentence—a great big topic sentence. By the third passage, every hand in the room went up when Amy asked, "Who can tell me the main idea for that passage?"

Then came passage four. The main idea was not in the first sentence. It wasn't in the last sentence. It wasn't in any sentence at all. It was an idea that had to be gleaned by putting together events from different sentences. The kids read the passage and hands went up. Amy called on a kid. The kid, very predictably, identified the first sentence of the passage as the main idea.

"Well," Amy said. "That's one of the things that happened. But what's the whole main idea, the whole main idea?"

With resolution, kids went back to the passage to find that elusive whole main idea. It must be here somewhere.

More hands went up. One belonged to a kid who identified the last sentence as the main idea. Another belonged to a kid who read the first sentence **and** the second sentence. After each kid's efforts, Amy said, "Yes, that happened, but what's the **whole** main idea?"

Not one kid in Amy's class figured out that the main idea was to be synthesized from the events described in the passage. But the kids were surely not to blame; nor was Amy. The **curriculum** caused the problem by implying that the main idea was the first sentence of a passage. It presented three examples of this form. Understandably, the kids assumed that main idea was a sentence game and that the main idea was the first sentence of the passage. From their standpoint, this was the message conveyed by the material. If main idea was not to be interpreted this way, why didn't the program present a counter example earlier?

The problem with the program is technical. The infraction, however, is caused by a lack of empathy. Amy's program is designed from the standpoint of adults, designed to appeal to adults. The program does not view instruction from the viewpoint of a naive kid.

Fixing up the instruction involves presenting a very careful sequence of examples and presenting explanations that are relatively unambiguous. The wording of these explanations is very important. If the teacher talks too much, the kids will have trouble identifying what's important. If the teacher uses non-functional expressions, such as referring to the "whole main idea," kids won't really understand what she's trying to say.

There are different solutions to solving this problem of effective communication. One is to try to train the teachers to be effective curricular designers. To the best of my knowledge, this has never been done, and for good reason—it would take several years of intensive training to make teachers effective. Another solution is to control what the teacher says by scripting it. This is the approach that we use in designing programs. We provide verbatim wording for the teacher to follow. The script specifies the examples that are presented to the kids and exactly what the teacher is to say when presenting each example. On the surface, this solution may seem restrictive. Actually, it works quite well. The teacher doesn't have to spend hours planning a lesson. Everything is there. The teacher should rehearse the lesson so that she presents in a lively manner. She should be fluent enough with the script so that she can observe what the kids are doing and respond to them appropriately. But the solution is effective because it reduces preparation time and it assures that the kids will not be zapped with confusing presentations, confusing examples, or confusing language.

A program that is scripted is very up-front about what is being taught and how it is being taught. The up-front presentation lets the teacher see just how much practice it takes to develop particular skills over time and what kind of practice is effective.

The tightly designed program also makes teacher training feasible. The program provides a sequence that will work if presented appropriately. If the kids are appropriately placed in the program, the program has the potential to teach all of them, on schedule. Conversely, if the kids are not being taught on schedule, some teachable aspect of the equation is not in place. The core teacher training simply focuses on all those aspects of the teacher's presentation and interaction with the kids that could foul up the teaching—pacing, reinforcement, challenging, correcting errors, and managing. This scope is incredibly smaller than the scope we would have to deal with if the teacher made up the instructional sequence and taught it (or even made up the "corrections"). In fact, it would be difficult for us to work on relevant teaching behaviors in situations like Amy's where the curriculum is sloppy. Before we could work on any teacher-presentation skills, we'd have to redo the curriculum so that it had the potential to work.

We train student teachers at the University of Oregon. Much of what they learn is provided through practica. As a rule, it takes about a month for the student teacher to become proficient at the mechanical aspects of presenting the script-pacing, following the wording, stressing important words, clearly signaling when the kids are to respond, and other mechanical details. We spend the rest of the school year working on interacting with the kids—correcting mistakes effectively, anticipating problems, reinforcing kids, challenging them to work hard, and dealing with a variety of "behavior" problems.

Providing this type of training for the typical teacher in the typical district is not usually possible—even if they are committed to following scripted presentations. The schools have neither the structure for effective supervision nor the training program. Given the difficulty of effectively training teachers to use highly structured programs (which is relatively easy), imagine the impossibility of training teachers who are using whole language or are trying to teach reading through "literature." The difficulties are so overwhelming that the responses of school systems are predictable. The decision makers simply don't specify what the kids are supposed to learn. The teacher is reassured that every child will learn something, but we don't know what that will be. The system may adopt an "ungraded primary" to further obscure the fact that neither teachers nor administration has a sensible teaching plan. The curriculum is now off the hook. So the teacher can be let off the hook. If we don't know what the kids are to learn, we can't fault the teacher for not teaching it, and we don't have to torture ourselves over trying to design teacher training that is effective.

An alternative to this retreat from performance standards is to design programs that will work, but design them in a way **that relieves the teacher of even more responsibility for communicating with the kids**. Possibly, instruction could be designed so it provided not only the examples and the sequence of examples, but also communicated directly with students, and presented in a way that had appropriate pacing, inflection, and the other details that make a difference in the fidelity of the message.

The teacher would be responsible only for managing the kids and reinforcing them for working fast and accurately. The program would do the rest.

In 1982, Alan Hofmeister, then Dean of the Graduate College at Utah State University, approached me and several of my colleagues about such a plan—designing instructional programs for videodiscs. Hofmeister had done a lot of research with laser videodiscs and had arrived at the conclusion that the videodisc had unique capabilities for delivering super instruction. A TV set shows the material and delivers the narrative. The discs are capable of presenting "movies" or "animations," and also still frames. Furthermore, the disc technology permits the design of lessons, quizzes, tests, reviews, remedies—everything needed for teaching a particular topic.

The teacher wouldn't have to present and therefore learn high-powered presentation techniques. The teacher would monitor the kids, determine whether they need more practice on particular skills and (by pressing a couple of keys on her remote-control device) direct the program to repeat part of the lesson or present additional problems of the type the kids were having trouble with. This plan would take us as close to instructional magic as we'd probably ever get.

At the time Alan first contacted us, news of the *A Nation at Risk* was casting gloomy shadows over the high-school and college scene, particularly in areas of math and science. As always, reforms were in the works. Alan had interested a recently formed enterprise, Systems Impact, Inc., in the promise of laserdisc technology for solving some of the at-risk problems. We were also excited about the prospect of being able to work with a medium that would require less dependency on the teacher as a presenter.

The original programs scheduled were in physics, chemistry, and algebra. None of these programs got past the initial development stages, however. The first program we developed for field tryout was beginning algebra. For a field tryout we needed a prototype of the program; however, we couldn't create a videodisc program. So instead, we hired a couple of our more talented trainers to make a video**tape** prototype, which lacked much of the sophisticated video techniques that would appear in the finished version, and also lacked a lot of the precise timing. But it had a reasonable sequence of tasks and examples.

Chapter 8: Effective Training

We had prepared the initial 15 lessons of the algebra program based on what we assumed the kids knew. Unfortunately, our estimates were mistaken. As part of the pre-test for the tryout group, we presented a series of problems that involve simple addition, subtraction, and multiplication of fractions.

When we tabulated the results of the pre-test, we knew that we might be in deep trouble. Of the 32 junior-high kids in the tryout group, one could add fractions with unlike denominators:

$$\frac{2}{3} + \frac{3}{4} =$$

One kid in the group could multiply fractions:

$$\frac{2}{3} \times \frac{3}{4} =$$

Unfortunately, the kid who could add was not the kid who could multiply.

The video had been prepared, so we didn't have a lot of choice but to launch into the program. After about four lessons, we added some hastily made material dealing with fractions. We pushed ahead, slowly, to lesson 12, but at that point, it became apparent that the only thing to do with these kids was to bring them back to frame one and teach them about the properties of fractions and basic fraction operations. Their misconceptions were amazing. Some of them could tell whether a fraction was more than one or less than one; however, they didn't seem to understand that the **1** referred to is the same **1** you say when you count: **one**, two, three…

We looked at some other "pre-algebra" groups and observed the same problems we saw with our group. So we scrapped the algebra program and started over about ten rungs lower on the academic ladder, with fractions, what they are, and how they work.

From a design standpoint, videodiscs make a lot of sense. They show dynamic changes and relationships that are not easily illustrated with static pictures. For instance, they can show that two fractions, such as $2/3$ and $4/6$, are equivalent by rolling a "pie" illustration of 2-thirds over the illustration of 4-sixths. The colored areas are the same size, so the fractions are equivalent.

Also, the videodisc narration can be very elegantly coordinated with the video. The narrator says, "When the top number of this fraction gets larger…," and just as the words come out, the top number starts changing to larger numbers. When the narrator refers to the parts of the fraction—the top number or the bottom number -the parts referred to are highlighted in time with the narration.

The video program also makes it possible to present instruction in lumps that are easily digested. Instead of going on and on about a particular topic (à la PBS programs) the videodisc can provide a short explanation, lasting no more than a minute or two, during which the narrator shows how to work a particular operation or handle a particular discrimination. Then, the narrator says something like, "Your turn…" The live segment stops and a still-frame problem appears on the screen, with instructions. After the kids work the still-frame problem, the teacher simply presses a button on the remote-control device, and the correct work for the problem appears on the screen.

Quizzes and tests can be designed so they are followed by a simple menu that indicates which "chapters" in the program provide appropriate remedies for particular problems kids have with various parts of the quiz or test. The teacher assesses the number of kids who missed items in a part of the test and determines whether a remedy is needed. If one is needed, the teacher presses a couple of buttons on the remote device and within two seconds, the remedy begins.

All these attractive capacities give the medium great potential, but without good, carefully designed instruction, all the flashy video and the clever features of the program will flop. The medium is not magic, a lesson that should have been learned from the schools' abortive and costly love affair with computers.

Many districts committed heavily to the promise of CAI (computer assisted instruction). The problem was that most of the software was just this side of pathetic, relying largely on bleeps, gimmicks, and other funsy cutesy devices to make the machines "user friendly." They weren't friendly. Except for a remarkably few software packages, the instructional sequences were sophomoric.

In over 90 percent of the cases, the software packages were in complete disuse—gathering dust—within four months of their purchase date. And the computers all but ceased to be used for CAI. Instead, the computers became "word processors" and "spreadsheet" designers.

Whether the medium is a text or a computer, the design of the instruction overrides all other factors, including individual differences in kids. On the question of instructional design and its relation to individual differences, James Brophy concluded in a paper he presented in 1986, "Research has turned up very little evidence suggesting the need for qualitatively different forms of instruction for students who differ in aptitude, achievement level, sociometric status, ethnicity, or learning style."

Brophy's statement doesn't imply the kind of fantasy that California claims "for all kids" in their pursuit of meaning. Some kids need more practice exercises than others. Some will take more time to accumulate the skills needed to enter a particular program. But if the program does an effective job of communicating with the kid, showing exactly what to do and providing adequate practice for the kid who needs more practice, the program is a good program for **all** kids who have the skill assumed at the beginning of the program.

Most educators would howl in disagreement over Brophy's assertion that learning styles and individual differences have a relatively minor effect on kid performance. Traditional educators stress the importance of "individual differences" and learning styles. Fortunately, one feature of the videodisc programs permits research that can answer the question: How important are these differences? That feature is the highly refined teaching sequences. If Brophy is correct, these sequences should prevail and even lower performers should do well, regardless of their learning style.

Several such studies were conducted using the videodisc programs. My favorite compared the performance of "learning disability" high school students and "remedial students" who had failed previous science courses to the performance of advanced-placement students who were in their second year of chemistry. This study was done as part of the initial field-testing of our videodisc program on *Chemistry and Energy*. The learning-disability kids and remedial kids went through the videodisc sequence, after which they and the advanced-placement kids were tested on bonding, equilibrium, energy of activation, catalysts, atomic structure, and basic properties of organic compounds. Although the advanced placement students were light-years ahead of the video group in achievement (close to the 90th percentile in math and science), the remedial students outperformed them **on every topic**, and even the learning-disabled students outperformed them on bonding and equilibrium. The mean post-test scores for the video group was 75, compared to 71 for the advanced-placement students. Brophy is right.

Other questions concerning teacher performance can be answered by the video programs. Because the programs handle a large segment of the total teaching, the relative importance of the teacher's behavior when presenting the videodisc lessons can be assessed. Some of the questions that can be answered are:

- How well does the average teacher manage kids?
- How much training does the average teacher require to follow a set of steps for interacting with kids?
- How much difference in kid performance results from presenting the video program different ways?

Those in the "scientific" camp would predict that if the teacher presents the lessons in the sequence as designed and doesn't deviate from sensible behavioral rules, the kids will learn more and learn faster. The traditionalists would suggest the teacher should adapt and adjust the program to the needs of her students.

The videodisc rules for managing kids are actually fairly simple. Here they are for the math programs:

1. Do not present from the front of the room. Use your remote and circulate among the students as the video presentation is going on and when students are working the still-frame problems.

Chapter 8: Effective Training

2. Model the responses you expect from the students. When the narrator asks a question, answer it. Reinforce students who answer.
3. When students are working still-frame problems, direct them to follow the instructions on the screen. Do not "reteach" or explain things that were presented during the live segment of the video.
4. Reinforce students who work quickly and accurately.
5. During the early parts of the program, be very strict about mechanics. Students are to write the problems exactly as specified. Don't permit them to omit signs, omit specified steps, or deviate from the solutions that are shown on the screen.

You would think that any certified teacher would be able to follow those directions and would know why they should be followed. Unfortunately, a fair percentage of teachers have learned to do things in a way that is at odds with the stated rules. For instance, rule 3 says that you shouldn't reteach and give a lot of individual help. The reason is simple. The kids who come into the program typically have gone through traditional sequences where they "discover" and make up rules. They don't understand how things in math actually work, and one method they have used in the past is to ask the teacher to show them how to do things. The bottom line is: If the teacher responds to calls for individual help when using the video program, the class will soon experience a contagion of helplessness. If the teacher tells the kids, "Do what it tells you to do on the screen," and reinforces kids who do it correctly and quickly, the kids' behavior will change. They will become more self-reliant, and they will succeed.

One videodisc study addressed a couple of questions:

- What kind of training or classroom monitoring is needed to make teachers effective?
- Is the performance of the kids really correlated with what the teacher does? (If the teacher doesn't follow the management rules, do the kids perform as well or nearly as well?)

Eight teachers of learning-disabled kids attended a two-hour training session during which the trainer demonstrated how to use the equipment, explained the classroom set-up, and went over the management rules, indicating why each is important and what is likely to happen if you don't follow it. The trainer also stressed that a goal was to shape up the kids so they could move quickly through the program, because the faster pace keeps them on task better and also gives them a better idea of the concepts that are being taught.

Following the orientation, all the teachers were observed, but only four of them received feedback, demonstrations, and help from the trainer in the classroom.

The results were interesting. The best teacher at following the management rules was a teacher in the workshop-only group. And guess whose kids had the highest scores at the end? Hers. They achieved over 90 percent mastery on the material.

Which teacher was the worst in following the rules? Another teacher in the workshop-only group. His kids did the worst of any group. They mastered 60 percent of the material.

The other two teachers in the workshop-only group were marginal—not disasters but somewhat below adequate. Their kids scored in the low 70 percent range.

In the group that received classroom monitoring and feedback, all the teachers performed adequately and their kids performed adequately, in the 80 percent range. So, enforcement of the rules was correlated with kid performance. The study suggested that a fairly high percentage of teachers need hands-on management training and feedback to implement the management rules. The typical workshop of two hours is not adequate to give this information to the average teacher, even if the workshop is very specific and provides practice exercises.

Another type of research possible with the videodiscs compares different approaches to the teaching of something like fractions or ratios. Several studies of this type have been conducted. In one conducted by investigators at Vanderbilt University, videodisc instruction in fractions was matched against a program developed by Nashville public schools. A large number of classrooms was involved in this study. Most of the kids already had some knowledge of fraction operations, but the groups were reasonably well matched in what the

Chapter 8: Effective Training

kids knew. The results: kids in the video program increased their skill by about 30 percent. During the same time the kids in the Nashville program increased by eight percent.

How important are instructional-design details of the programs? An interesting study was done to assess these factors. Two teachers used an overhead projector to present examples that precisely matched the sequence of examples shown on the video program. They also read the same script the video narrator presented. Of course, it took them approximately eight hours to prepare for each lesson, and it took two of them to manipulate all the material needed to present each lesson. But by following the same wording and presenting the same examples in the same sequence, they achieved the same results with their kids. There were no differences between kids who received the videodisc program and those receiving the teacher-presented program. In other words, the instructional design of the material—not the medium—makes the difference.

Another intriguing feature of the video sequences is that they are so effective if presented according to the rules that they can be used as something of a standard by which to evaluate other methods. For example, the current trends in math instruction promoted by organizations like the National Council of Teachers of Mathematics (NCTM) are based on the use of manipulatives, immersion in "problem solving," and the general belief that if kids are involved in working with math and numbers, they'll somehow become proficient at math. A scientific approach to instruction would say: No way.

Bonnie Grossen conducted a great study that provided an idea of just what "No way" really means. She worked with two teachers. One was a devotee of manipulatives and the NCTM approach. This teacher spent lots of time teaching math—1½ hours a day. She gave her students big time homework assignments. She worked until eight every evening preparing for the next day. The other teacher did not believe in homework (yea for her). She spent far less time on teaching math.

This study was great because the kids (6th graders) were matched in performance, and pairs were randomly split for distribution to the two classrooms. The resulting classrooms were greatly heterogenous. In the end, the "NCTM" group was slightly (but not significantly) above the video group.

After both groups worked on fractions, decimals, and percents for a semester, they received a three-part test: the first part on tasks and problems that were unique to the video program; the second on the tasks and problems unique to the NCTM program; the third on tasks and problems common to both programs.

The results: The lower half of the videodisc group outperformed the upper half of the NCTM group on everything. On the items presented only in the NCTM program, the lower half of the video group averaged 65 percent correct; the upper half of the NCTM group averaged 51 percent correct. On those items that were common to both programs, the lower half of the video group averaged 65 percent correct; the NCTM group averaged 35 percent correct. The upper half of the video group averaged 90 percent and 97 percent on these two parts of the test.

Clearly the problem of providing effective math instruction has far less to do with the kids than with the delivery of instruction.

While the "research" that's possible with the videodiscs may be important to help resolve some of the theoretical nonsense that characterizes traditional education, the primary function of the videodiscs was to serve an incredible need. Since the publication of *A Nation at Risk*, swarms of "reforms" buzzed through the educational community, but nothing happened.

Obviously, we felt that the videodisc programs would catch on as solutions to the most basic problems that preempt kids (including girls and minorities) from moving into science and math, but they did not. In a lot of districts, the programs were not adopted because they ran counter to adopted district guidelines or scope-and-sequence stipulations. Typically, a math supervisor or a group of teachers "evaluates" the video programs and concludes something like this: "We don't teach improper fractions that way." Or, "We don't teach the skills in the same order as the videodisc program. Some are taught in the third grade, some in the fourth. So we can't use the program. It doesn't fit in with our scope-and sequence." Or, "We don't like the use of terminology in this program. The person speaking refers to the top number and the bottom number of the fraction. We refer to them as **numerator** and **denominator**." Or, "Our teachers feel that a great deal of adaptation would be required to make this program appropriate for our setting."

First consider the circularity of dealing with schools. If the programs were designed so they taught everything the way the schools do it, the program would get the same results the schools get, which means that it would fail. But if the programs were designed in this way, they would be acceptable to the schools. Unfortunately, the program can't be effective and also acceptable.

Next, consider the district guidelines. They become the standard- the basis for determining how and when things will be taught. This situation would be perfectly reasonable if the district guidelines had been demonstrated to work and if the district had only minor problems teaching kids. When the facts of failure are legion within a district, however, the guidelines become effective only in feeding the sorting machine. The district is saying in effect, "We don't know how to teach the skills consistently (witness our failure rate); however, we have specified guidelines that indicate when things are to be taught and how they are to be taught. We will not permit any variation from these guidelines."

If you try to point out that there are a lot of kids who are failing and the programs can help them, the response is often circular. "Our new guidelines are designed to correct that problem, and that's our current mission." Trust me, the **new** guidelines are probably no more capable of improving the situation than the **old** guidelines.

Another problem with the video programs is their cost. As of this writing, a three-disc program costs $1800, which seems like a big bundle. In the context of the schools, however, the cost is relatively trivial. Consider a teacher whose salary and benefits may cost the district $45,000 a year, and consider the "cost effectiveness" of that teacher if the kids are not uniformly learning. Part of this cost effectiveness involves "reteaching" the kids in later grades, remedial programs, and the like. (About 70 percent of most 6th-grade math basals are devoted to **review** of material taught in earlier grades.)

Within this context, the videodisc expense is relatively small, particularly since the program has a long life expectancy and can be used by more than one teacher. (All that's needed is a cart to transport the videodisc player and related gadgets from one classroom to another, and a schedule that permits the targeted subject to be taught at different times in different rooms.)

Alan Hofmeister pointed out that a single computer station can accommodate no more than 15 students a day, whereas the video-disc program can teach 150 kids a day. On the subject of computers: the cost of a videodisc program is actually much less than it would be if the same program were in a computer. You'd need almost 1000 floppy discs to create what's on a three-disc program. Even if you left out the animations and replaced them with static pictures, you'd be looking at about 35 discs.

I find the expense issue tragic. Many parents put aside large sums to send their kids to college. Too bad the schools don't have a similar savings plan.

In some ways, the videodisc programs represented our most frustrating rub with the schools. I could see the enormous changes that would be required for schools to teach programs like DISTAR Arithmetic, which requires a lot of presentation skill. But I had, and still have, trouble understanding how products that meet the needs of effectively teaching math and science, that require a relatively small effort from the teacher, and that are very successful with just about all the teachers that have used them appropriately, could fail to catch on.

CHAPTER 9
THEORIES

Traditional educators simply love theories. However, their literacy about theories is very low, which means that they try to apply theories to instruction that have either very limited implications for instruction, or none at all. The educators' typical approach is to find out some fact about kids. The fact may involve demography, learning style, neurology, psychology, development, or whatever. They then borrow, adopt, or make up a theory that relates this fact to what should be done in instruction. Naturally, their plans fail, and fail big time. The failure is easily predicted for one simple fact: After you make your theory that connects learning to some other characteristic, such as developmental trends of children (brain-growth spurts or the like), you still have to design an instructional program that exploits this revelation.

Consider the notion of learning styles, which was popular in special education in the '60s before many studies suggested it was perfect nonsense. Some kids are identified as visual and some as preferring or learning better through the "auditory" modality.

So what do you do about this interesting fact? Do you "strengthen" the auditory capacity of children who are primarily "visual"? If so, you need an instructional program. So now you have something of a detour through the brain. The kid is failing in reading or math. You present your program that is supposed to strengthen "auditory perception." The program is either a success or a bust. For the sake of argument, let's say that the program is a complete success. The kid can now hear a pin drop on the other side of the city. The kid has such phenomenal auditory acuity, that he has to wear ear muffs most of the time to keep from getting over-whelmed from auditory stimulation. Can he read any better than he could? Or perform any better in arithmetic? No. Strangely enough, he must still be taught all the things in arithmetic or reading that he didn't know before this incredible "perception" training. But with his phenomenal auditory ability, will he learn much faster than he would have without the auditory training? Maybe a tad,

Chapter 9: Theories

but no evidence exists to suggest that it amounts to much. The auditory training was a waste of time because it didn't address the central problem the kid had in the first place.

We gave the training the benefit of the doubt because we assumed that it would be a smashing success; however, traditional educators should not be permitted this benefit. The reason is that they are naive **about instructional design**. They don't understand details—how many trials would be required to induce particular behaviors, what reasonable options are available for presentation formats, how the material can be organized so that less teaching is required to induce desired generalizations, or how to address any of the hundreds of technical details that make the difference between good instruction and junk. Therefore, they are largely victims of slogans and very global notions.

The educators' major problem, however, is that they are fundamentally looking for magic. The California Department of Education suggests that many kids already know how to read when they enter school. Let's assume that this assertion is accurate. But let's say that we're faced with a first-grade classroom full of kids who seem to be developmental aberrations. None of the kids seems to know how to read. What do we do now? How has our quaint little fact about development helped us teach the kids? It hasn't. In fact, all it's done is what it was probably intended to do in the first place, which is to provide us with sorting-machine information. At the end of the year, after we have diddled around with these kids and exposed them to the search for meaning, we can say, "I know that they didn't learn to read, but they were below the developmental norm when they entered school."

Again, the information about development suggests a detour in designing instruction. The kids are developmentally behind. The traditionalist provides a program that is supposed to "accelerate" the kids' development, to make them "ready to learn" or provide some such global benefits. So now somebody has to design an instructional program to do that. The program is implemented. Even if it succeeds (making kids extremely ready), the kids still can't read.

The avant-garde group most preoccupied with these displaced labors and logic is composed of "cognitive psychologists." "Cognitive psychology" describes phenomena you already know. The phenomena are simply embellished with fancy labels such as "metacognition," "schema," and so forth. Cognitive psychologists are masters at detours, and they often confuse cause and effect. They may observe that the kids who are good readers view homework differently than poor readers. Their approach wouldn't be to teach the poor readers to be good readers and then see the extent to which their attitudes about homework change. Instead, they would try to change the **attitudes** about homework and then see if they read better. Even if kid attitudes do change, what possible benefit derives from the instruction? So now, the kids who are poor readers just love homework as much as they love books. Instruction is still needed to improve their reading. If the reading problem had been addressed directly, the kids might still hate homework. At least they would be able to do it.

In summary, the problem with cognitive information, neurological information, or the kind of stuff you may read in *Psychology Today*, is that the remedies or procedures used by the school are supposed to be instructional, which means that they **cause** predicted changes in the kids' behaviors. If the "cognitive" information is treated as the focus of this instruction, we must use two instructional programs; the first to tune up the learner's cognition, the second to teach the kids the stuff we were supposed to have taught in the first place. Of course, some "theorists" argue that if we install the first program, the second will happen automatically. Unfortunately, there is no data to suggest that this will happen. By pumping kids up so they have a "positive self-image," we don't really help them learn arithmetic if the arithmetic lessons provide the kid with a lot of information that would puncture anybody's positive self-image.

A far superior plan is: Teach the kids how to do math well and along the line they will most certainly develop a good self-image about math.

Lauren Resnick, who is often quoted by the new wave of "meaning-oriented" educators, provides some nifty examples of the contorted logic that is currently in vogue among "cognitivists" or "constructivists" as they like to be called. In a recent chapter that she wrote, "Teaching Mathematics as an Ill-Structured Discipline," she argues that math teaching should be based on discussions and disagreements. Resnick's argument opens with the obvious fact that kids are poor in

Chapter 9: Theories

math and exhibit, "general inability to use mathematical knowledge for problem solving." No argument here, except possibly on the point of whether they have relevant mathematical knowledge that they need for "problem solving." It would be a little taxing to work a problem that required manipulation of fractions if you didn't know what fractions are or how they work.

Resnick's approach to solving the problem-solving dilemma begins with some of those fascinating cognitive facts and correlations (none of which generate much information about instruction).

> Good readers…do more elaboration and questioning to arrive at sensible interpretations of what they read…good reasoners in political science and economics…and good science problem solvers…all tend to treat learning as a process of interpretation, justification, and meaning construction. As in these other fields, students who understand mathematics as a domain that invites meaning construction are those most likely to become flexible and inventive mathematical problem solvers.

From these fascinating correlations, Resnick draws conclusions:

> All of this suggests that we urgently need to begin investigating possibilities for teaching mathematics as if it were an ill-structured discipline. That is, we need to take seriously, with and for young learners, the propositions that mathematical statements can have more than one interpretation, that interpretation is the responsibility of every individual using mathematical expressions, and that argument and debate about interpretations and their implications are as natural in mathematics as they are in politics or literature.

In summary, kids are unable to use mathematical knowledge in problem solving; good performers in different subjects interpret and justify; therefore, we should treat math as an ill-structured discipline, assume that mathematical statements can have more interpretation, and somehow promote argument and debate.

If you're able to follow this argument you either are, or think like, a cognitive psychologist. (For what it's worth, I think the argument came about because Resnick tripped over a few synapses while wandering through kids' brains.) Although it may be possible to argue that statements of math, such as $4 + 2 = 6$ may have more than one interpretation, the argument wouldn't go very far. Possibly, Resnick is confused about the difference between the interpretation of the statement and the ways in which it might be represented. It can be represented with counters, number lines, claps and an indefinitely large set of events that can be "counted." But its interpretation remains pretty monolithic.

Resnick is trying to argue from "language" to math, but it won't work because statements of math are basically different from those of "language." The question, "Where is the man?" has thousands of possible answers because there are thousands of possible settings for the man. The questions: "How many plus two equals six?", "Four plus how many equals six?", and "Four plus two equals how many?" have only one answer each (in base 10 systems). Math ain't language.

Certainly people may have different ways of mentalizing math. One kid remembers four plus two by thinking of a number line. The kid next to him remembers it by thinking of the second counting number after four. There are any number of possible internal pictures that a person may have for organizing information or relating it. These are as irrelevant as the fact that if you read the sentence, "The man was standing," you may get a picture of a particular kind of man. So long as you know that your image is consistent with the sentence only in the **important details**, it's just a peachy image and it's all yours. Everybody has their own.

Resnick's next point is that when math expressions are applied to "the actual things in the world to which abstract mathematical entities can be reliably mapped," we "encounter an explosion of interpretations." Not really. We encounter an explosion of possible applications. Three dogs plus two dogs equals five dogs. We can picture long-tailed dogs or short-tailed ones. That's our choice so long as we picture dogs, not blocks or snakes.

After apparently convincing herself that all the questions to be answered lie in the kids' head and that "there is no single meaning for a mathematical expression," Resnick conducted some "experiments." The first was to ask "French middle-school children to make up stories

Chapter 9: Theories

that could be represented by expressions such as 17 - 11 = 4 or its equivalent." The goal was to "use children's knowledge of the relationships between stories and expressions to help them understand the reasons for such symbolic algebra rules as the 'sign change rule'."

Things didn't work out too well. "We never reached the algebra goal, however, since many of the children were not able to relate arithmetic expressions reliably to stories."

Time out: We seem to have some ground shifting here. At the last checkpoint, Resnick was going to teach mathematics as discussion and debate. The goal of this project, however, was apparently not to teach mathematics, but to teach some dippy "understanding." For Resnick to perform her magic, she apparently needed kids who had **knowledge of mathematical expressions** and **knowledge of word problems** and **knowledge of how to relate the two**. From that, she would teach them all they ever wanted to know about sign rules. The kids didn't have all the knowledge that Resnick had hoped for, so the experiment was a flop. But wouldn't this have been a splendid opportunity for Resnick to show the validity of the debate-and-discuss approach to math by teaching the kids the **knowledge** they lacked? In fact, if her approach does not induce mathematical knowledge, how can it be considered an approach at all? Stated differently, how are the kids supposed to acquire the mathematical knowledge they lack?

Following Resnick's sign-change-rule fiasco, she picked up the questionable fact that naive kids discussing things figured out answers to problems "even when both discussants begin at the same low level." This was apparently a breakthrough. Possibly, kids don't have to understand math if they can discuss it. As Resnick put it, "The importance of this finding is that it eliminates the possibility that a more advanced child simply taught a new response to a more backward child." (She has such a way with words.) "Instead, something in the conflict of opinions apparently sets constructive learning processes in motion."

Armed with this speculation about teaching, Resnick et al. launched into a study involving "socially-shared" problem solving. Resnick asserted that this endeavor presents difficulties to the experimenter, one of which is that "children frequently come up with incorrect formulations that do actively interfere with problem solving." Isn't that amazing? If kids don't know how to translate the math story problem into an appropriate "formulation," they don't come up with the right answer (unless they make some other mistake along the way).

The experiment may have been frustrating for Resnick et al. When kids worked collaboratively on word problems involving fractions, they would do such nerdly things as drawing a "pizza divided into six parts, shade three parts, and then assert that each shaded part was 'a third'."

Anyhow, the experimental team discovered that it could not present problems associated with what the kids were supposed to be learning in the current school year, because they typically didn't have the math knowledge needed to solve the problems. So the team presented problems based on skills taught in earlier grades. The kids received coaching in discussing problems. Kids had different roles as they worked "collaboratively" (planner, critiquer, etc.).

Still no brass ring. As Resnick put it, "And while children discussed the roles a great deal, they did not become adept at performing them."

A change in the structure of group interactions provided the "critic" with cue cards that prompted questions such as "Why should we do that?", "What do the numbers mean?", and so forth.

The results? "Nevertheless, at the end of 13 sessions, there was no strong evidence that the overall level of problem-solving activity has improved substantially."

Gracious.

The final attempt of Resnick et al. in working from the kid's mind outward to the curriculum involved three pairs of children at each grade level from four through seven. Each pair received varying amounts of training in using a "planning board" for figuring out "What we need to know." (One pair received no such training; one received "minimum training"; and one received maximum training.)

The problem Resnick et al. reported involved a "stereotyped" word problem of the sort that Resnick decries. The problem involved Mark shopping with some friends. He bought various items, sold his pen to

Chapter 9: Theories

a buddy, found a quarter, counted his money at the end of the day and discovered that he had $4.43 left. The question: "How much money did he start out with?"

So here were the kids working in pairs (or dyads), using their "planning board," and figuring out how to solve this problem. How many of the "dyads" did it correctly? None. Not one pair of kids got the correct answer—no controls, no minimum-training dyads, no maximum-training dyads, no fifth graders, sixth graders, or seventh graders. Undaunted, Resnick observed that "most of the dyads located the difficult aspect of the problem but did not resolve their questions successfully."

If you're keeping score, the only reasonable conclusion Resnick et al. should draw about their series of foozles is that structuring math as an "ill-structured discipline" didn't seem to be very productive at anything.

It didn't teach any math. It didn't improve the kids' ability to solve problems even when they could work in pairs and receive the support of the other kid in the dyad. The discussions didn't seem to set "constructive learning procedures in motion," or provide the medium that permitted individual kids to transcend their "backwardness." About the only thing the kids could do was make stupid comments about three-sixths being a third, ask **rote questions** that are prompted by cue cards, and bumble around with discussions over a problem that any sixth grader should have been able to solve without a planning board or the support of a dyad partner.

Possibly the most revealing comments in Resnick's chapter follow her somewhat unabashed discloser that no "dyads" succeeded. "Our present data do not follow dyads for long enough periods to track changes in specialization but we can show how our analysis would lead us to determine such specialization." Indeed, Table 5 did show just how Resnick et al. would have analyzed the role changes associated with "specialization." I don't know why anybody would be interested in doing this, unless they strongly believed that the unstructured-discipline orientation was like a life-form that had to survive. In her last section, Resnick seems to confirm this stance. "If we want students to treat mathematics as an ill-structured discipline—making sense of it, arguing about it, and creating it, rather than merely doing it according to prescribed rules—we will have to socialize them as much as to instruct them."

This conclusion seems to have dropped from one of the epi-heavens. Resnick didn't show us that anything approximating important learning occurred from what she apparently thought were activities that permitted kids to make sense of the topics. Furthermore, Resnick provided the kids with "prescribed rules." Granted, the rules had to do with using the planning board, but they were rules. Resnick's plea for socialization is pretty hollow. Socialization is nothing more than acquiring specific behaviors and receiving a lot of practice in applying these behaviors to appropriate situations. In instructional circles, we refer to this notion as teaching.

To traditionalists, instruction is the poor stepchild of psychology. Actually, instruction is the proving ground of theories. And the history of applying theories to this setting shows clearly that most psychological theories don't lead to exemplary practices. Most cognitive theories are too broad to suggest the specific detail that must occur in the instructional setting. An example is "schema theory."

Several years ago, I was asked by Robert Floden, associate director of the National Center for Research on Teacher Education, to write a paper. The idea was for Floden to write his paper—the flagship paper—on what teachers need to know about learning. Then another minor leaguer and I were to explain our respective positions. When I talked to Floden on the phone, he explained that his paper would be on "schema theory," which was a currently modish position used by places like California to support slogans about the search for meaning being the central business of learning. I explained to Floden that I thought schema theory wasn't a theory in any reasonable sense of the word, and that it didn't provide teachers with any specific directions about what to do. He indicated that he still wanted my input, which he somehow thought was "strictly behavioral." I don't understand exactly why. Doug Carnine and I had written a book titled *Theory of Instruction* that is based on the idea that many major aspects of instructional design or curriculum development can be achieved analytically, without reference to kids or even behavior.

Chapter 9: Theories

In any case, Floden promoted schema theory as the key to training teachers.

What is schema theory? That's hard to say. According to Floden's paper, "When pupils engage in the tasks of school, they try to fit what they are experiencing into their current knowledge and understanding; that is, pupils make sense of instruction in ways that depend on what is already in their minds. Psychologists use the concept of schema to organize what they know about human perception, learning and memory."

If this description means that kids would be preempted from understanding if they lacked knowledge that was **logically** needed to make sense of the message, the question doesn't need a theory to explain it. Quite the opposite. A theory would be needed to explain how anything else could be true. For instance, we present a kid with this sentence: **Four tramgards of herpsils approached the grumole**. The kid who is knowledgeable about English knows that four sub-types of something approached something else, but that's all that's logically possible, because the rest of the nouns are not known to the kid. Therefore, the kid is preempted from understanding the sentence in more specific detail. It's impossible. The mind might guess, but that's not knowing.

If we give the kid information about different "unknown" words, we provide the kid's mind with the information it needs to make more sense of the sentence. If we tell the kid that a **tramgard** is a group of ten, that a **herpsil** is a soldier, and that a **grumole** is a river, we will have provided the kid with the information needed to understand the sentence fully (assuming that the kid understands **ten**, **soldier**, and **river**). Four groups of ten soldiers approached the river.

If kids could understand the sentence without background knowledge, they would provide evidence that ESP is very real, but they would raise a question about why kids who learn one language don't understand all of them.

Floden made some reasonable observations, such as the idea that because pupils know different things than teachers do, pupils' interpretation of instruction may differ from what teachers **intend**. But the most important point is not stated, which is that the kid's interpretation will almost always be based on the curriculum as it was presented to that kid.

Floden presented an example involving a fifth grader named Benny, thought to be doing well in math by his teacher. However, a "researcher interviewing Benny was surprised when he claimed that 1.2 was the same as ½." Benny's explanation was that answers are considered correct only if they match the answer key.

Floden referred to several other examples. One involved kids not really understanding what they learned about the earth being round; another involved how to avoid possible confusions kids might have when they are introduced to a unit on photosynthesis. These examples provide the only places where Floden's notion of schema theory touches ground, and the examples are very edifying because they show whether or not Floden knows the cause of the problems or how to fix them. Although he apparently doesn't understand that the curriculum is the cause of the problem, he sees the teacher who understands schema theory as the solution. He maintains that these teachers will be more likely "(a) not to assume that satisfied pupil faces mean that pupils have learned what the teacher hoped they would learn, (b) consequently, to do more to probe the understanding of at least a sample of pupils..., (c) to attempt to take pupils' current knowledge into account in planning instruction, and (d) to assume that, because students may have different schemata, they will have to represent the subject matter in more than one way."

Notice the assumptions: If the teacher spends time probing, the teacher will identify the problem. Then the teacher will be able to "plan instruction" around pupil misconceptions. The teacher will somehow be much better than Amy was at correcting these problems of misconception.

Unfortunately, Floden didn't provide evidence that he knows how to do it. For Benny (who thought that ½ and 1.2 were equivalent), Floden provided no specific remedy. For the flat earth, no remedy except to provide the questionable advice that the teacher must make the children "dissatisfied" with their current schema, apparently by pointing out problems with what they currently believe. Floden cautions, however, "To get pupils to switch to the appropriate organizing framework, the teacher must make this seem attractive." I'm sure the teacher will know how to do that.

For photosynthesis, Floden does make some concrete suggestions. Here's the first:

> The teacher with no understanding of how schemata change might simply explain the process of photosynthesis to the students, perhaps using experiments to make the need for light vivid. The teacher with an understanding of how schemata change, however, will begin by finding out what pupils believe. If they believe that water and soil are food for plants, the teacher might do an experiment that demonstrates that plants grown in the dark soon die. The teacher would then try to create discomfort with the initial beliefs by pointing out to the pupils that the plants had plenty of water and soil.

This proposed experiment, of course, is a perfect disaster. It's supposed to show that water and soil could not be food. In my response to Floden's paper, I wrote:

> Obviously, the experiment doesn't show that at all. We hope that there are no smart kids in this classroom because just one of them could raise havoc with this "demonstration." The kid brings in three dead plants. He explains, "I took the first one out of the soil and put it in distilled water, in sunlight. It died in a few hours. I used a hair-dryer to dry out the soil in the second one. I put it in the sun. It died in a few hours. I took the third one, pulled it out of the soil, laid in on the dry ground, in sunlight. It died right now."

So if Floden's experiment (showing that a plant dies in darkness) is supposed to prove that water and soil are not food, the kid's experiments would seem to prove that sunlight is not "food" either. After all, the kid's plants had plenty of sunlight; yet they died—and very soon.

But is the plant grown in darkness dying? According to Floden it dies soon, but alas, he's wrong. (It may live for months, depending on its dormancy responses, and it most probably will be growing like crazy. The reason is that sunlight inhibits stem growth. Remove the sunlight and the stem grows like a bandit.) So the experiment is a perfect disaster. The idea of creating discomfort is a slogan, a notion that another cognitive psychologist proposed. But he never demonstrated that "discomfort" activities are efficient or even necessary in the instructional arena.

Floden's biggest problem has to do with his curriculum. Smooth learning cannot take place unless curricular details are in place, and Floden's conception of photosynthesis is problematic. He asserts that "starch stored in the roots or seeds **is** food," and that "plants, like animals, need food to provide energy for growth and the operation of the systems of the organism." Wrong. Plants do not need food, and certainly the stuff they store is no more in the category of "food" than your fat and muscles are. (It might be "food" for some other organism, but certainly not for the plant.)

Obviously, kids might become confused about food if they are in a program that treats the component parts of the plant as "food," and insists that plants "make their own food." In fact, plants are like animals in that both need sources of energy and raw materials that can be converted into chemicals that give up energy. We use "food," oxygen, and water. Plants use sunlight and chemicals that are in the air or soil. All done. No big schema problems.

Floden's remedies are paradoxical because they assume that what the kids learn is influenced or caused by what the teacher does. (Otherwise, what's all this business about creating dissatisfaction in kids?) It follows that the curriculum is the core to the solution. A poor curriculum communicates misconceptions—inappropriate "schemata." A good curriculum doesn't. Floden's specific solutions are naive because he tries to solve the problems that kids have without addressing the primary cause—the curriculum.

The unfortunate aspect of the energy educators spend on theories is that it represents a greatly displaced effort. The theory assumes the pose as the "generator" of important practices and techniques. Actually, the theory provides very general rules, not the specific detail needed for designing lesson 12 of a curriculum. We could design lesson 12 so that it is consistent with schema theory and so it worked very well with the kids. Or we could design lesson 12 so that it was consistent with schema theory and flopped. We could do the same thing with most theories. We could make them look good or look bad. But regardless of how they look, the action is in lesson 12, not in the theory. If educators focused more on the facts and details of lesson 12, they'd be a lot smarter about their business.

A corollary is that school board members, parents, and the business community shouldn't be intimidated by educational theory, but they also should be concerned with lesson 12 and all its cousins. If they concern themselves with accurate facts of student performance and require the administration to do the same, they can promote a much more responsible use of "theory" in education

CHAPTER 10
MATH MADNESS

Math instruction in our country is a mess, and the mess results largely from decisions made by educators in the '70s. A very popular notion in the '70s was "discovery learning," which produced poor results when compared to more structured methods. Discovery, however, was a built in component of the "new math." Educators loved the notion of "discovery," because it was based on a theory that became very popular in the late '60s–the developmental theory of Piaget. According to this theory, very young children do mental operations that are internal representations of concrete actions. The kid manipulates something concrete and observes the outcome. Later, this action becomes internalized and the kid is able to do things mentally that had been achieved earlier only through manipulation.

The most unfortunate aspect of Piaget's theory is that it is irrelevant to instruction. Piaget insisted that "learning is subsumed by development." In other words, if you want to talk about learning, you must **first consider development**. This qualification tends to make the theory irrelevant to "teaching," where the game is to induce learning right now.

In any case, the post-sputnik math programs, particularly in the early grades, were so bad that universities have had to lower their standards greatly to accommodate even the better performers in math. The last ten years have been peppered with studies that document the failure of our kids to learn math. One of the more thoughtful reports was *The Underachieving Curriculum*, which was published in 1987. The report is based on an international comparison of kids in grades 8 and 12 on different math topics. The results followed the now-familiar pattern of showing that our kids fell well behind Japan, France, and Hong Kong at both grade levels. Our eighth graders were in the middle of the twenty-country pack in "arithmetic" (10th place), somewhat farther behind in algebra (12th place), and near the bottom in geometry and measurement (16th and 18th place). The twelfth graders did worse.

They were second from the bottom in algebra, fourth from the bottom in functions and calculus, and third from the bottom in geometry.

The Underachieving Curriculum went beyond crying over the poor showing of the U.S. kids to an analysis of why our kids perform so poorly. The authors considered possible explanations about why our kids were failing and ruled out all but one of the possibilities.

The first possibility is that there isn't sufficient time allocated for instruction in math. Wrong. The U.S. kids in the eighth grade received 144 hours of instruction per year, compared to 101 hours for kids in Japan and 120 for kids in Hong Kong. (Both these countries shred us in international competition.)

Possibly our classes are too big. Wrong. Our average class size for eighth graders is 26 kids; in Japan and Hong Kong, over 40 kids are in a class. (These countries have about the same size classes for advanced math, while the U.S. has classes that average 20 kids.)

Certainly, we educate a higher percentage of kids than they do in those other countries. Wrong again. 82 percent of our kids remain in school; Japan retains 92 percent.

Possibly teachers are more poorly prepared. *The Underachieving Curriculum* didn't think so, at least not in terms of things that could be counted, such as years of training. The report noted, however, that Japanese teachers tended to blame themselves if their kids failed, while U.S. teachers were far more likely to blame other factors—the home, student attitudes, and the like. Paradoxically, U.S. teachers reported that mathematics was rather easy to teach. Japanese teachers indicated that it was difficult. Possibly, there's a great big difference in the teachers' conception of what teaching is.

After considering the various factors that could contribute to the performance of U.S. kids, the report observed:

> In the various critiques of U.S. education, the curriculum has received relatively little attention. Yet we believe that data from the Study provide convincing evidence that the mathematics curriculum deserves careful scrutiny and attention during this time of concern for educational renewal. In its

goals, in its strategies and in its expectations for students, the Study has shown the U.S. schools mathematics curriculum to be underachieving.

The general design of the curriculum used by traditional educators is referred to as a spiral curriculum, which was popularized by a cognitive psychologist, Jerome Bruner. According to Bruner, the basic

> ...ideas that lie at the heart of all science and mathematics ...are as simple as they are powerful. To be in command of these basic ideas, to use them effectively, requires a continual deepening of one's understanding of them that comes from learning to use them in progressively more complex forms.

So far, Bruner's conception seems reasonable. Bruner's ideas, however, were not shaped by an understanding of instruction, but rather by developmental theories like those of Piaget. So the method Bruner recommended for achieving this "continual deepening of one's understanding," was the spiral curriculum. "A curriculum as it develops should revisit these basic ideas repeatedly, building upon them until the student has grasped the full formal apparatus that goes with them."

Translated into practice, the spiral curriculum is a series of different, unrelated topics that parade past the kids year after year. Kids dabble in measurement for a while before moving on to the next unit, which may be geometry, which is followed by whole-number operations, which is followed by fractions,...and so forth. Typically, about 60 school days pass before any topic is revisited. Stated differently, the spiral curriculum is exposure, not teaching. You don't "teach" something and then put it on the shelf for 60 days. It doesn't have a shelf-life of more than a few days. It would be outrageous enough to do that with one topic—let alone all of them.

Bruner's endorsement of the spiral curriculum suggests the extent to which cognitivists lack a comprehensive schema of a kid's brain. Don't they know that if something is just taught, it will atrophy the fast way if it is not reinforced, kindled, and used? Don't they know that the suggested "revisiting of topics" requires putting stuff that had been recently taught on the shelf where it will shrivel up? Don't they know that the constant "reteaching" and "relearning" of topics that have gone stale from three months of disuse is so inefficient and impractical that it will lead not to learning but to mere exposure? And don't they know that when the "teaching" becomes reduced to exposure, kids will understandably figure out that they are not expected to learn and that they'll develop adaptive attitudes like, "We're doing that ugly geometry again, but don't worry. It'll soon go away and we won't see it for a long time"? Apparently not, even though it would take very little time working in a classroom to document all of the above.

The Underachieving Curriculum judged that the problem with the spiral curriculum is that it lacks both intensity and focus. "Perhaps the greatest irony is that a curricular construct conceived to prevent the postponing of teaching many important subjects on the grounds that they are too difficult has resulted in a treatment of mathematics that has postponed, often indefinitely, the attainment of much substantive content at all."

The report recommended a curriculum that was more "blocked" or "sequential" so that it would be possible to establish "clear expectations for achievement prior to moving on to the next substantial body of mathematics."

Possibly the most serious mistake *The Underachieving Curriculum* made was to present "propositions" for change. Most of these propositions seemed eminently sensible, such as establishing "clear standards for achievement," re-evaluating "the role of textbooks as curriculum guides," and reconsidering "early sorting of students into curricular tracks that lead to vastly different opportunities to learn high school mathematics."

One of the propositions, however, seems to have rung the traditional educator's bell:

> **The content of the mathematics curriculum needs to be reexamined and revitalized**. The domination of the lower secondary school curriculum by the arithmetic of the elementary school has resulted in a program that, from an international point of view, is very lean. The curriculum should be broadened and enriched by including a substantial treatment of topics such as geometry, probability, statistics and algebra,

as well as promoting higher-level process goals such as estimation and problem-solving.

Math educators apparently felt compelled to respond to broadening the curriculum, and their response is just what you would expect—a travesty. The quintessence of "reform" came from the National Council of Teachers of Mathematics (NCTM) in the form of the organization's 1989 *Standards*.

The *Standards* opens with a statement of the problem and the great inequities that exist. It pledges to redress these inequities.

Here's part of the opening:

> Mathematics has become a critical filter for employment and full participation in our society. We cannot afford to have the majority of our population mathematically illiterate. Equity has become an economic necessity.

Those words spark a sense of purpose and commitment. The Standards also offer consumers of math material protection:

> Schools, teachers, students and public at large currently enjoy no protection from shoddy products. It seems reasonable that anyone developing products for use in mathematics classrooms should document how the materials are related to current conceptions of what content is important to teach and should present evidence of their effectiveness.

But what is the evidence for the effectiveness of the recommendations provided by the *Standards*? A report by NCTM's Research Advisory Committee was published in 1988, prior to the *Standards*. This document pointed out that the draft version did not indicate which recommendations "were based more on informed judgment or personal opinions of the authors…"That's a kind way of putting it. Bishop's critique of the published *Standards* put it this way: "Recommendations and exhortations appear to be supported only by opinion—authoritative opinion, it is granted—but opinion nevertheless."

For an organization that proclaims to protect all of us against shoddy products, the NCTM would have to present "evidence of effectiveness" based on a field-test of all of the *Standards'* recommendations, or

Chapter 10: Math Madness

at least clusters of recommendations. Since the *Standards* provide no such documentation, the NCTM's posture as the protector of public interest is presumptuous.

Bishop suggests that the opinions are authoritative. I doubt that, particularly when the *Standards* feature Resnick as a cornerstone of their recommendations and start with some pretty questionable premises. For example:

> Instead of the expectation that skill in computation should precede word problems, experience with problems helps develop the ability to compute. Thus, present strategies for teaching may need to be reversed; knowledge often should emerge from experience with problems. In this way, students may recognize the need to apply a particular concept or procedure and have a strong conceptual basis for reconstructing their knowledge at a later time.

How can kids solve the problems intelligently unless they have the computational or conceptual knowledge they need to work the problem? Resnick's kids couldn't do it. They were preempted from working any kind of problems related to what they were currently being taught because they didn't know the math and therefore struck out on the problems. The experience with the problems did not produce magical concepts.

One more point: The notion of equity doesn't match up well with this notion of "deep water" learning. We know, before we start, who will fail to learn from immersion with "problems." And of course it will be those kids who are featured in the emotional plea for equity.

The *Standards* go all out for manipulatives, so much so that the teacher of the "model classroom" in kindergarten through 4th grade would probably need several assistants and a large inventory list to keep track of the various pieces.

> Classrooms should have ample quantities of such materials as counters; interlocking cubes; base-ten, attribute, and pattern blocks; tiles; geometric models; rulers; spinners; colored rods; geoboards; balances; fraction pieces; and graph, grid, and

dot paper. Simple household objects, such as buttons, dried beans, shells, egg cartons, and milk cartons, also can be used.

The NCTM's recommendations for activities in grades kindergarten through grade four are apparently based on the moral commitment that: "Problem solving must be the focus of school mathematics."

This commitment is guided by a suggested insight into learning: "Programs that provide limited developmental work, that emphasize symbol manipulation and computational rules, and that rely heavily on paper-and-pencil worksheets do not fit the natural learning patterns of children and do not contribute to important aspects of children's mathematical development."

The *Standards* present some activities that illustrate this thoughtful marriage of the commitment to problem solving with insight about kids' mathematical development.

Here's one: The teacher tells the kids, "I have some pennies, nickels, and dimes in my pocket. I put three of the coins in my hand. How much money do you think I have in my hand?"

We're not sure about the grade level at which this activity is appropriate because the *Standards* don't deal in that sort of specificity. About the only guideline they provide is the statement that for kids to develop problem solving abilities, "Students need to work on problems that may take hours, days, and even weeks to solve."

Maybe the three-coin problem is one of those problems that takes weeks. I can certainly see it taking weeks in the second grade. And I can see the kids getting a little tired about being told that they are wrong. One kid says, "Twenty cents," and the teacher says, "Wrong."

Another kid says "Twenty-one cents," and the teacher says, "Wrong." Some of the other kids look out the window and wonder when this problem solving will end.

The *Standards* seem to think that mathematics is an "ill-structured discipline." "Exploring, investigating, describing, and explaining mathematical ideas promote communication. Teachers facilitate this process when they pose probing questions and invite children to explain their thinking." Isn't that what Resnick's kids did?

Chapter 10: Math Madness

Another thoughtful activity demonstrates that three-word problems can be represented with the same set of counters. For all three problems, you start with 14 counters and subtract five. I'll bet the kids, particularly fourth graders, are just bursting with developmental excitement the third time they have to lay out the same set of counters and do the same operation they just did two times. I'd almost bet that the teacher could present another one of those stimulating word problems and the kids could do it without even listening to the problem.

Here's a fascinating puzzle suggested by the *Standards*:

> Who am I?
> I have three or four sides.
> All my angles are equal.
> My sides are not all equal.

I know of no three-sided figure in ordinary three-dimensional space that meets these criteria. (The first clue says that it's possible for this form to have three sides or four sides. Bad.)

The *Standards'* orientation to math derives pretty directly from Piaget—"informal exposures," followed by internal representation.

> Children need extensive informal experience with problem situations and language prior to explicit instruction and symbol work with operations. Thus, informal experiences with all four operations should begin in kindergarten and continue through grade 4. Instruction should help children connect their intuitions and informal language to operations, including the mathematical language and symbols of each operation...Time devoted to conceptual development provides meaning and context to subsequent work on computational skills.

But let's consider one of the *Standards'* conceptual "problems"—one that sets the stage and prepares the little guys for the formal world of symbols and signs.

> Anton, Juanita, and Booker want to share six cookies equally. How many cookies does each one get?

I suppose the drama could be conducted with either real cookies, milk cartons, dried beans, or some of the more formal counters. (I wonder if it screws the kids up conceptually if they have to represent cookies rather than work with the real thing. If they don't actually get to eat the cookies will this experience no longer be truly concrete, but possibly only quasi-concrete and therefore incapable of being "internalized"?)

Once the nature of the counters has been settled, the kids could work in teams. Maybe each team could be composed of someone who plays Anton, Juanita, and Booker. The teacher puts out the six cookies the kids are to share equally, and the kids act it out and connect their intuitions and informal language to operations. The teacher observes that most of them are getting it right! According to the *Standards*, children should share their solutions. So let's see what they learned to guide them to a more abstract understanding.

> "What about you, Anton? How did you figure it out?"
>
> "One for me, one for her, and one for Booker. One for me…"
>
> "Now, can you tell me something about the size of the number you started with and how that relates to the number of cookies each of you has now?"
>
> "We had six cookies. Now we each got two."
>
> "So now they are divided equally."
>
> "Yes, one for me, one for her, and one for Booker. One for me…"
>
> "Yes, what operation would you say this problem is based on?"

Long pause.

> "Well, would you say that it's addition, subtraction, multiplication, or division?"
>
> "Division," Juanita says.
>
> "No," Anton says. "It's addition. I counted out. We didn't have any. Then, one for me, one for her, and…"
>
> "No," Booker says. "It's subtraction. You took those cookies off that tray and here they are, but there's none on that tray."

Chapter 10: Math Madness

There's a very simple reason that explains why manipulatives will never consistently work in teaching basic mathematics conventions and notations. The reason is this: While the manipulative activity is consistent with a particular mathematical operation or notion, it is also consistent with other possible interpretations.

The "cookie sharing" experience is consistent with the operation of division and consistent with the notation:

$$\frac{6}{3} = 2 \quad \text{or} \quad 3\overline{)6}^{\,2}$$

However, nothing within the "experience" guarantees that the kids will focus on this aspect of the acting out. They could act out many similar "division" problems and never learn the relationships that are assumed by mathematical notation. So long as they apply the one-for-me-and-one-for-you operation, they don't need to learn anything more, and many of them won't.

The same problem exists with all manipulatives. Kid play with rods that represent different values—based on the length of the rod. Kids can use these rods to perform a variety of "act-outs" that are **consistent with** complicated math notions, such as the idea that 10 x 2 equals 5 x 4, but the kids doing the acting-out are typically not learning this relationship. They're simply making one group of rods the same length as the other group. The great meanings that they're deriving are not in their minds but in the imagination of the educational observer.

Direct work with the symbols and notations of math is a far safer method of teaching relationships because symbols are consistent with far fewer misinterpretations than noisy and often time-consuming act-outs. The *Standards* do not favor pencil-and-paper work, however, because such work implies skills, and the *Standards* are very ambivalent about skills.

> Premature expectations for students' mastery of computational procedures not only cause poor initial learning and poor retention, but also require that large amounts of instructional time be spent on teaching and re-teaching basic skills... Children should master the basic facts of arithmetic that are essential components of fluency with paper-and-pencil and

mental computation and with estimation. Children will need many exploratory experiences and the time to identify relationships among numbers and efficient thinking strategies to derive the answers to unknown facts from known facts.

In another place, the *Standards* indicate:

Some calculation, if not too complex, should be solved by following standard paper-and-pencil algorithms. For more complex calculation, the calculator should be used (column addition, long division).

So it seems that such things as "long division" are really too difficult. In another place, however, the *Standards* indicate:

It is important for children to learn the sequence of steps—and the reasons for them—in the paper-and-pencil algorithms used widely in our culture. Thus, instruction should emphasize the meaningful development of these procedures, not speed of processing.

So, do we or don't we? And how much if we do? After each suggestion that something might have to be **taught** to the children, the *Standards* follow with a reiteration that exploratory experiences are the name of the game. "Although the exploration of computation with larger numbers is appropriate, excessive amounts of time should not be devoted to proficiency."

I think that what the *Standards* folks are trying to say is, if your kid can tell you something about how long division works, that's good enough. If the kid can't carry, that's peachy so long as she has a calculator.

Mostly, however, the *Standards* avoid actually thinking about the kid as a changing entity who grows in knowledge. All activities for the "primary grades" are assumed to be wonderful experiences for kids who are five, six, seven, eight, or nine years old. Any parent knows that nine-year-olds are a lot different from five-year-olds. It doesn't matter to the *Standards* because many suggested activities are inane for kids of any age. Consider the following primary-grade recommendation as it would apply to a class of fourth graders (nine- or ten-year-olds). "Pretend we own a children's shoe store. We need to know

123

Chapter 10: Math Madness

whether to have more cloth or more leather shoes for sale in our store. What could we do to decide?"

You might think that the answer would lie in calling a shoe store, or consulting a reliable source. No.

> The children might decide to make a floor graph with one shoe from each child as a way of determining the number of cloth and leather shoes in their class. Questions to guide students' activities can include these: Are there more cloth shoes or leather shoes? Are the two numbers close? Should we have about the same number of cloth and leather shoes in our store?

Cute. A classroom full of one-shoed fourth graders taking possibly 10 minutes to set things up so they can answer those mind-stretching questions. I'll bet the kids stay on task, particularly if a couple of the kids have a dirty sock, stinky feet, or holes in their socks.

The juxtaposition of suggestions in the *Standards* is sometimes frightening. On the same page as the shoe-graph are the semi-monthly temperatures for different cities (January through March). One of the cities, of course, is Sydney, and one of the questions, of course, is: "Why do you think New York is getting warmer and Sydney is getting colder?" If these kids are being taught science the same way they are being taught math, they wouldn't have a clue, because they have had no hands-on manipulative experience with Sydney. (If you can't represent shoes by counting them, how could you begin to deal with a place as far away as Sydney?) Consider the incredible difference in the questions asked, "Are there more cloth shoes?...Why would it be getting colder in Sydney?" They seem to represent both ends of something. But they share a feature—the format of presentation. What if a kid actually answered the Sydney question? Instead of saying something like: "That's the way it was last year. We had that big cold spell during spring vacation," the kid says this: "Sydney is in the southern hemisphere. New York is in the northern hemisphere. During our winter, the sun's rays hit more directly below the equator. So, Sydney is having its summer, while New York is having winter"? One kid answered the question. But what about Anton, Juanita, and

Booker? Did they learn something from that explanation? Chances are they didn't.

The *Standards* superficially responded to the various propositions of *The Underachieving Curriculum's* request for more probability and statistic. According to the *Standards*, that shoe-graph activity and the one involving guessing the number of cents the teacher has with three coins are probability statistics activities.

But the primary plea from *The Underachieving Curriculum* was for an overhaul of the curriculum so that it abandoned the spiral curriculum and provided something far more sequential and intensive. It cautioned:

> Any new organization of curriculum should increase the intensity of content coverage and establish clear expectation for student attainment. Definite accomplishment milestones and leaving points need to be established in order to minimize the lingering of unmastered content from year to year.

How did the *Standards* respond to this qualification? Obviously, it didn't. It identified the topics that should be presented in the primary grades: whole number computation, geometry and spatial sense, measurement, statistics and probability, fractions and decimals, and patterns and relationships. But it did nothing to erase the spiral curriculum. In fact, the spiral curriculum lives if the teacher is to expose kids to these topics. So far as the clear expectations for student attainment, there are none—no guidelines for grade-level markers and such a complete lack of concern with sequence that kids in grades K through grade four are treated as a single entity. The *Standards* apparently see no contradiction in teaching "probability" or fractions to kindergarten kids who may not be able to count to 20.

The Underachieving Curriculum called for a serious reform. The *Standards* responded with a redefinition of math as an unstructured discipline. The *Standards* de-emphasize anything teachers have failed to teach. According to the *Standards*, "pencil-and-paper computation cannot continue to dominate the curriculum or there will be insufficient time for children to learn other, more important mathematics they need in the future." Like what? The kids in high school who are failing in math and who can't perform on the level of kids in Hong Kong, or even Canada, are failing tasks that involve pencil-and-paper computation.

The Underachieving Curriculum called for promoting goals such as problem-solving, and the *Standards* proclaim that the central focus of math instruction must be on problem solving. However, *The Underachieving Curriculum* was obviously concerned with the fact that kids don't know how to solve word problems or similar problems that have substance. The reason kids don't know how to solve these problems results largely from the fact that there is no teaching. How has the *Standards* responded? Their solution is simply to retreat to manipulatives—beans and cartons—and to act-out activities that do not address the actual problem but serve more as a hope that Anton will learn something.

The most serious problem with the *Standards*, however, is its arrogance. In the tradition of the sorting-machine, it assumes that it can derive a curricular reform through metaphysical masturbation of words, not through experimental evidence about what works and what doesn't. The writers of the *Standards* did not verify these activities, suggestions, and standards by first demonstrating that they worked and that they created kids who performed well in math. Instead, they made it up and then presented it as an authoritative document.

The last section of the *Standards* presents an incredible suggestion that puts the *Standards* in perspective.

> One reviewer of the working draft of the *Standards* suggested the establishment of some pilot school mathematics programs based on these *Standards* to demonstrate that all students— including women and underserved minorities—can reach a satisfactory level of mathematical achievement and urged that the success of these students be widely publicized.

Don't these people recognize that the time to provide such a field-test is before the fact—even before the recommendations and suggestions have been written in draft copy?

I don't know about you, but I'd give the NCTM a great big F in problem solving.

Possibly, the most frustrating aspect of the trends in math are not that they represent a very transparent retreat from anything teachers had problems teaching, but that they present nothing new. The manipulatives, the exposures, the acting-out, and the moral insistence on "problem solving" has been a theme of math educators since the mid '60s. The approach is actually one of the reasons kids currently don't know long division and are not proficient at paper-and-pencil work in math.

In 1981, Doug Carnine and I sued the Oregon State Textbook Commission for not adopting *DISTAR Arithmetic*. The reason the commission didn't adopt it was that it didn't meet the criteria the commission had established. And the criteria were cut from the same cloth as the current NCTM standards. Programs were supposed to promote "friendliness" with numbers, and there was to be an emphasis on "problem solving."

Although *DISTAR Arithmetic* has lots of word problems (as part of nearly all the lessons in the program), the Commission rejected *DISTAR* on grounds that it lacked "problem solving."

We lost the suit, but the proceedings were enlightening. Unlike the suit in California, this one permitted courtroom drama—witnesses, cross examination, and all those good things. So it was possible for us to scar up the Commission in the courtroom. The most outrageous episode in the case occurred on the last day of the trial. The Commission based its rejections of *DISTAR* largely on the evaluation of the program by a consultant, considered an expert in math education, Dr. Oscar Shaaf. He had taught at the University of Oregon, served as math coordinator for several school districts, carried out research projects funded by the National Science Foundation, and lectured widely on the topic of his NSF study—problem solving.

On direct examination, he explained very expansively how he wanted to see kids measure the gymnasium with tongue depressors and then with paper clips, so they would learn about measurement.

Our strategy on cross-examination, was to pin Shaaf down on "problems," and how they cued mathematical operations. The idea was to start with a simple word problem like this one:

Chapter 10: Math Madness

Jane has four oranges.
Then she buys three more.
How many does she end up with?

This is problem type occurs repeatedly in the early levels of *DISTAR* because it provides kids with a map for translating the sentences into mathematical symbols.

Jane has four oranges. The starting number is 4.

4

Then she buys three more. She buys three more so she adds three.

4+3

How many does she end up with? The how many is an unknown amount—a box. **Ends up with** is an equal sign.

4+3=☐

The problem has been translated into a statement of arithmetic. The kids now apply a counting operation. The equal sign tells them that both sides must have the same value. Kids count and figure out how many are on the side with 4 + 3. The same value is transposed to the right side. All done.

The points that we hoped to make during the cross-examination were:

1. These are perfectly legitimate "problems" for beginners.

2. To translate the problem, kids have to understand what the different sentences imply and how they translate into symbols.

3. Therefore, before kids work these problems, they should be taught the various "translation skills," as well as the computational procedures.

4. Once kids have a model of these simpler problems, it's very easy to introduce more difficult variations.

Unfortunately, we were not able to pursue all those points under cross examination. The text that follows explains why. It is an unedited transcript of the trial record, as it appears in the Lane County, Oregon, records. The questions are posed by our attorney, Evelyn Thomas. The answers (such as they are) are provided by Oscar Shaaf.

Q. On the problem…"Jane has four oranges. Then she buys three more. How many does she end up with?"…do specific words in the problem tell how many she has at first?

A. Will you read the question again? I didn't…I didn't remember all the details, I should say.

Q. "Jane has four oranges. Then she buys three more. How many does she end up with?"

A. The total number is not stated in the beginning. Is that your question?

Q. I just asked, do specific words in the problem tell how many she has at first?

A. Well, I guess not. I don't know what the point of the question is.

The COURT: Well, now, that doesn't have anything to do with you, Doctor. The question is: Can you answer it or not? Whether you understand the point of it or not doesn't make any difference.

The WITNESS: I can answer a question and give an answer to the problem, yes, if that is what she wants.

The COURT: Read it again. Read it again. Now, listen carefully.

Q. (by Mrs. Thomas) "Jane has four oranges. Then she buys three more. How many does she end up with?"

A. She has seven.

Q. That was the problem. Now, my questions is: Do specific words in that problem tell how many she has at first?

A. No. The—I don't know the point of the question. I mean—

Q. Specific words in that problem do not tell how many she has at first? Is that…

A. I don't know what is going on in your mind when you ask that question. I mean, I don't know what you are after. You are not communicating to me.

Chapter 10: Math Madness

The COURT: Well, you are not supposed to read her mind. Ask the question again, and either tell us "yes," or "no," or "I can't solve it." Go ahead. Ask the last part again.

Q. (by Mrs. Thomas) Do specific words in the problem tell how many she has at first?

A. Would you read the problem again?

Q. "Jane has four oranges. Then she buys three more. How many does she end up with?"

A. It tells you how many she had in the beginning. I wanted to check to see if that was correct.

Q. How would "Jane has four oranges" translate into a numerical problem?

A. The numbers in the problem were "six" and "three." I would say six plus three is equal to nine.

The COURT: Wait a minute. Wait a minute. Read that problem over again.

Q. (by Mrs. Thomas) "Jane has four oranges. Then she buys three more. How many does she end up with?"

A. Four and three.

The COURT: Now, we are going to have a recess. If you are going to take four and three and get nine, we have got to have a recess.

(Recess taken.)

The COURT: You may proceed.

Q. (by Mrs. Thomas) Doctor Shaaf, I was posing a possible problem, "Jane has four oranges. Then she buys three more. How many does she end up with?" And I asked you, do specific words in the problem tell how many she has at first?

A. Yes.

Q. Okay. How would "Jane has four oranges" translate into a numerical problem?

A. Four plus, I believe it was three, is equal to seven.

Q. Okay. I'll ask you just the…how would "Jane has four oranges" translate into a number?

A. Four.

Q. Okay. The next part says, "Then she buys three more." Now, how would that part translate into a number?

A. Three.

Q. How do you…okay. And how do both parts…okay. You said, "four plus three." How do you know that you are going to add?

A. When you read the problem to me, it suggested a setting and it suggested to me a setting that was addition. As far as exactly what specific word suggests that to me at this time, since I…I mean, I don't remember the wording exactly.

Q. Okay. The last part of the problem says, "How many does she end up with?" How would that translate into a numerical operation?

A. I imagine "four plus three is equal to seven."

Q. Now, if you were a student who has no pre-knowledge of arithmetic and if you had to perform the steps that you just went through to translate the story problem into a written problem, would that process be reasonably classified as a rote act?

A. I wouldn't say it was particularly rote in that case. There is a matter of interpretation of the words.

Q. And isn't it true that you cannot solve the problem unless you know what the words mean and how they might translate into a numerical operation?

A. You can solve it without that by acting it out and counting.

Q. You can solve the problem without knowing what the words mean?

Chapter 10: Math Madness

> A. That's right. You can solve and get seven. Kids in preschool before they have any instruction can get the answer of seven by acting it out and then counting.
>
> Q. If I understand you correctly, if someone posed that problem... "Jane has four oranges. Then she buys three more. How many does she end up with?,"...are you saying that a child could solve that problem without knowing what those words meant?
>
> A. They could solve the problem by...I mean, the "four" and the "three" and getting "seven." The students would get the answer. They don't have to worry about it being a mathematical sentence to get the answer.

You may wonder why Shaaf seemed to find the questions so difficult to answer. It would be speculative, and possibly dangerous, to try to imagine what he was thinking, but a possible inference is that he finds it difficult to think along the same lines as the questions. When the attorney asks, "Are you saying that a child could solve **that** problem without knowing what those words meant?", Shaaf fails to see that particular problem, with those particular words. For him, the problem apparently becomes confused with an entire group of problems involving counting out. Similarly, why would recounting the word problem or remembering the details of it be so difficult for Shaaf unless analyzing this kind of material was a perfectly unfamiliar activity for him?

The people who are making decisions about how math will be taught apparently share a lot of their premises with Shaaf and the NCTM. They see global things—kids manipulating. Their "vision" does not include facts about instruction. They are blind to the idea that a shoe-graph, although stupid in any grade, is stupider in some grades than in others. They fail to appreciate that instruction must develop concepts and skills. They see activities as ends, but any activity is simply a small part of a development, which may require several hundred carefully-sequenced activities to teach kids, not simply expose them. The decision makers are blind to basic instructional constraints: an activity must be effective with different kids; it must be **time efficient**; and it must be related both to what comes before it in the instructional sequence and what comes after it.

CHAPTER 11
GIVE THEM THE BUSINESS

In the spring of 1991, the results of the National Assessment of Educational Progress (NAEP) in math were released. California was in the lower third of all the participating states. The only states below California were Florida, Alabama, Hawaii, North Carolina, and Louisiana. When the results were released, Associate State Superintendent, Francie Alexander, expressed surprise. According to *Newsweek* (June 17), she said, "We've all been led to believe we were above average."

Her statement goes beyond irony. It indicates that the state did not have information about how students were performing. Although there are schools within walking distance in just about any California city, the State Department of Education allegedly didn't know that kids were failing miserably in math. The average for all states on the NAEP was very low, but the performance of California eighth graders was so low that well over half of them would qualify as being learning disabled in math. Only about 1 out of 12 (about 8 percent) could solve a problem like this one

$$\frac{2}{5} + \frac{1}{3}$$

Yet, Francie Alexander ostensibly thought that the kids were performing "above average."

Part of the problem may be the state's total disregard for data. California's Deputy Superintendent of Instruction, James Smith, wrote the editor of *Educational Leadership* on behalf of Honig and indicated why the State of California does not use "learner-verification data" and does not follow the statute that requires the State Board to use such data (section 60226). One point that Smith made was, "There is no requirement to do anything with the data – just receive it from the publisher."

The statute doesn't indicate that the State Board must use the data to make intelligent decisions about adopting instructional programs. But that fact doesn't really make Smith's observation any less irresponsible. Try to picture a State Superintendent of Public Instruction with values so contorted that he would have to be told how to use information that program A works and program B doesn't. Since Smith is so knowledgeable about the details of 60226 and how to get around it, he might have been able to figure out the big picture by reading the other statutes in the Education Code. They make references to improving effectiveness and efficiency of instruction. If Smith couldn't figure it out from those references, he at least might have asked himself, "Why do you suppose the legislature made up this requirement for the State Board to 'develop plans to improve the quality and reliability of instructional materials through learner verification?' "Are we to believe that Smith couldn't figure out the idea was to do more than just receive information from the publishers, or is it more likely that he and Honig have another agenda, and they are playing a rather transparent loophole game: "We're not going to use the data because you didn't tell us we had to. Ha! Ha!"?

The second comment that Smith made about "learner verification" is as revealing as the first. He indicated, "The State Curriculum Commission has found the information unreliable and of no use in the past."

This statement is a paradox. The purpose of the legislation was to "develop plans **to improve**" the material through learner verification. The call for improvement implies that the earlier reporting methods or bases for securing learner-verification data were not adequate. Smith seems to be arguing that improvement isn't possible or that the Curriculum Commission is infallible: The Curriculum Commission found data to be of no use; therefore, it's of no use and can be of no use.

The performance of California students in math provides some indication of the Curriculum Commission's fallibility. The 1985 Math *Framework* (designed by the Commission) provided the basis for how kids were taught math during the years 1985-1991. The 1985 *Framework* featured "teaching for understanding." It indicated that such teaching "takes longer to learn but is retained more easily... is difficult to teach...is difficult to test." The *Framework* emphasized "problem solving," and the role of the shadow teacher. "In problem solving the teacher should serve as a group facilitation rather than as a directive group leader..."Of course, the *Framework* emphasized concrete materials and Piagetian logic. "When students have internalized a concept through the use of concrete materials, they can move toward abstract representations of the concept."

The notions of heterogeneous grouping and negotiated learning were included. "When a cooperative climate has been established, small groups that are heterogeneous in their composition have the added value of promoting positive attitudes toward others, regardless of individual differences."

The 1985 *Framework* presented a timetable that indicated that in 1986 the state would "evaluate testing programs for consistence with the framework." In 1987-88 there was to be "ongoing evaluation."

The most revealing part of the *Framework* is its list of problems that would be presented as part of the eighth-grade curriculum. The *Framework* cautions that the list of more than 30 problems, "is meant to provide a few representative examples of the general level and approach of the course and is by no means complete."

One of the more ironic featured problems is:

> Write a set of directions for a younger student, explaining how to add ⅖ and ⅓. Then use a picture and write an explanation as to why you add fractions the way you do.

Remember, only about 1 out of 12 eighth graders could even solve this type of problem in 1990. (These eighth graders went through six years of school during which the 1985 *Framework* was in place.)

Some of the other problems presented in the eighth-grade curriculum are:

- Demonstrate that a terminating or repeating decimal can be represented as a fraction and vice versa. Use a calculator to compare decimal expansions of some rational and irrational

Chapter 11: Give Them the Business

numbers, with attention to the limitations of the calculator display.

- Obtain areas of regular polygonal figures and use figures inscribed in a circle to approximate π.

- Given the coordinates of a figure in the plane, rotate it through 180°, 90° or 45°. Translate it. Reflect it.

- Make a table, and sketch a graph of each function:

$$y = \frac{2}{5}x - 3 \qquad y = [x - 4] \qquad y = x2 - 5$$

$$y = x(x - 2)(x - 4) \qquad\qquad y = \frac{1}{x}$$

- What are the possible results of rolling two dice and subtracting the number showing on the face of one from that showing on the face of the other in such a way that a non-negative result is obtained? Guess which result is most likely. Try the experiment 50 to 100 times and record your results. Make a chart to find the theoretical probability of each outcome.

- Given the equation 5x − 7 = −3, prove, by justifying each step in the solution of the equation, that ⅘ is the only solution.

Given the obvious fact that not one California eighth grader in 1000 would be able to solve these problems, California bureaucrats and decision makers were provided with a discrepancy that is somewhat larger than a bread box. The *Framework* portrayed eighth graders who are eagles; the evidence shows that they were more like ground hogs. Either Honig, Alexander, and the rest of the state decision makers knew about this discrepancy, or they didn't. If they didn't, they should be in the running for the international irresponsible-administrators award. If they did know about the discrepancy and did nothing about it, they deserve the academic-child-abuse award. In either case, they deserve some kind of recognition.

There was supposed to have been assessment by 1987. If the assessment occurred, the results were not used to pull the plug on the plan, or even to let Francie Alexander (who in 1985 was acting Director of the Curriculum, Instruction, and Assessment Division) know that the plan was going belly up.

The 1985 *Framework* not only stayed in place, but it was referred to by the new *Framework* (1990 draft) as a model. The 1990 draft implies not only that the 1985 *Framework* led to acceptable results, but that it **also made teachers smart about teaching math**.

> We have a growing body of experience from teachers who have worked to achieve the goals of the 1985 Mathematics *Framework*, who have found that it is possible to avoid the pitfalls described above and to engage students in meaningful work.

No, Virginia, that's not the case. The 1985 *Framework* was a disaster; teachers and kids were permitted to fail year after year without one intelligent response from the state over the incredible amount of academic child abuse that was being created in the classroom; the key superintendents in the state and the people who authored the 1990 Math *Framework* ostensibly didn't even know that the kids were being punished by a curriculum that was light-years from their performance.

The facts about the 1985 Math *Framework* provide a good perspective for Smith's observation that the Curriculum Commission has found learner-verification data of no use in the past. Apparently the Commission and the rest of the state machinery find no data of use.

The state's latest math *Framework* is far more outrageous than the 1985 model. It calls for even more of what the 1985 *Framework* failed to deliver. The new *Framework* even argues that things do not have to be learned in a reasonable sequence. "A related misconception...is the belief that 'lower order' skills must be mastered before children are ready for 'higher order' skills. Again, the opposite is the case..."

Possibly, the biggest problem with this continuous saga is the response of the public and the business community to California decision makers. Francie Alexander was not run out of California for her contributions to academic child abuse. Honig is not recognized as a complete failure at proposing reforms or as an absolute nebbish at managing state machinery in a sensible way. In 1991 he appeared on the *MacNeil-Lehrer Report*. Lamar Alexander, Secretary of Education, pointed out that what we needed was more reform leaders like Honig. Honig indicated that he knows what needs to be done to solve problems of instruction, a puzzling assertion for someone who has never been involved in a successful demonstration and has proscribed any methods that permit him to receive data on what actually works. Another comment that Honig repeatedly makes is that it takes time for his plans to show results. He has made this comment about his newly installed middle-school program (which has never been verified to work any better than the earlier materials, but which was installed in 100 schools). How does this man know how much time it takes for results to occur if he has never field-tested the material and has no possible basis for determining a time line? Apparently, people who indicate "It takes time," are considered thoughtful individuals who are careful not to make outrageous claims. Ironically, Honig's claims that "It takes time" are more outrageous than claims about snake oil curing cancer. No amount of time is sufficient for his middle-school program to work.

For some time, the business community has been distressed with the soft minded practices that characterize education. Until recently, however, the attempts of business to influence the system have been benign, consisting mainly of gifts to school districts and projects that should have been left to die quietly. Recently, however, the business community has become more actively involved in educational reform. The principal players are: The New American Schools Development Corporation, The Business Roundtable, and local groups such as the Los Angeles based, LEARN (Los Angeles Educational Alliance for Restructuring Now). The most serious problem that the business community has in dealing with education is the credibility gap. Typically, the resolutions these organizations adopt are reasonable. For example, the Business Roundtable, which consists of 200 corporations (from American Express through General Mills and General Electric to Xerox), "supports the national education goals developed by President Bush and the nation's Governors." The Roundtable suggests that systemic change is needed and lists nine principles.

1. The new system is committed to four operating assumptions:
   - All students can learn at significantly higher levels;
   - We know how to teach all students successfully;
   - Curriculum content must reflect high expectations for all students, but instructional time and strategies may vary to assure success;
   - Every child must have an advocate.
2. The new system is performance or outcome based.
3. Assessment strategies must be as strong and rich as the outcomes.
4. School success is rewarded and school failure penalized.
5. School-based staff have a major role in making instructional decisions.
6. Major emphasis is placed on staff development.
7. A high-quality pre-kindergarten program is established, at least for all disadvantaged students.
8. Health and other social services are sufficient to reduce significant barriers to learning.
9. Technology is used to raise student and teacher productivity and to expand access to learning.

These principles are espoused by other business groups, like the New American Schools Development Corporation (NASDC), which is also committed to systemic change, alternative governance practices, and accountability. Its funding of promising plans for reorganized learning environments to achieve world-class performance standards is certainly an attempt to move in the right direction.

For all these groups, however, there seems to be a lack of understanding of what is needed to achieve results. The words are right. The ideas are right – in the global sense – but when they are applied to concrete situations, they lose their luster. For instance, the RFP (request for proposals) put out by NASDC had this comment about achievement measures: "While national standards will not be established until well into the design effort, existing curricular frameworks, standards, and tests may provide useful bases for designs. Examples include those proposed by such groups as the National Council of Teachers of Mathematics, the National Council of Teachers of English…"

I think the biggest problem groups like NASDC have is recognizing that virtually all the educators they will deal with on the reform level are naive about achieving results. The situation is typically different in business. We could solve a "business" problem that had never been solved by getting information, calling in experts, and the like. The solution is possible because the information is reliable and the experts are experts. For example, we have an irrigation problem in Nebraska. We can consult records to find out the level of the water table, changes over the years, the relative cost of various options, and we can make an intelligent decision on how to proceed. We can bring in an expert to refine details. If we are freed from needless red tape, we should be able to come up with a reasonable solution.

This model of securing information and formulating workable plans does not hold for education. The Business Roundtable supports site-based management. The assumption is that the schools have the same knowledge base that a trained engineer or manager would have. The assumption is that the staff would be able to understand the problem, know how to solve it, and know who could provide expert assistance. School staff members have no reliable tables or sources of information that tell them what can be done. Colleges of Education are bursting with professors who spout "research," "principles," and who advocate practices that will not work. Granted, there are some who would be reliable resources, but how does the school staff go about finding them? The state is not helpful in this respect. Most states, like California, simply support the latest "trends," which are nonsense.

The ultimate assumption of the Roundtable Principles, therefore, is that a group of school people who have never seen it done, who have never done it effectively themselves, and who know no effective consultants will be able to do it and do it well.

These organizations often compound the problem by bringing in educational consultants who have no first-hand knowledge of solutions. For instance, the California Roundtable commissioned Berman, Weiler Associates to provide the Roundtable with operating plans. Berman has been a marketer of trends for some time. If it's modish, Berman mentions it. As a colleague of mine put it, "He can argue for strict grade-level standards, for heterogeneous grouping of children, for direct instruction, and for whole language in the same sentence and with a straight face." The "plan" for the California Business Roundtable involves a pre-kindergarten for at-risk students; yet, academic work is to be delayed until children **reach 7 years of age**. This delay of academic work will simply widen the gap between kids who are ready and those who aren't. At the same time, it will obviously retard all of them.

So here's the California Business Roundtable, bristling with resolution about accountability and a new system that "is performance or outcome-based" espousing plans that aren't even second cousins to "performance-based" notions. Furthermore, the adoption process raises the question: Should accountability begin at home? Or, is the game simply to be do-gooders?

Several TV news shows have featured different programs and have presented the slant that the Roundtable merchandises, which is that if folks get their heads together, things will succeed. In 1991, *Prime Time Live* featured the Wesley Elementary School in Houston, Texas. The focus of the program was that the principal, Thaddeus Lott, did things his way in his school, and the students (black inner-city kids) outperformed the rest of Houston. Actually, a large part of the original force in Wesley Elementary school was the staff, led by Loraine Killion. In the 70s, Killion, through a scheduling quirk, moved from one grade to another with the same group of students. She taught those students with Direct Instruction programs. Killion was a star teacher. By the time her students (who had become officially known as Killion's kids) went into junior high, nearly every kid in the class qualified for Houston's gifted program.

During this period, non-reading kids came to Wesley School from all over the city. They were quickly converted to readers. The staff at Wesley was good; the practices worked. Other inner-city schools in Houston used the same instructional programs and practices Wesley

Chapter 11: Give Them the Business

school used, but when the administration chased new trends in reading instruction and mandated new practices, these other schools followed suit, even though there was a great drop in student performance. Wesley School, thanks to Lott, kept on doing what it had been doing.

So there's a mixed message. One is that Lott has great integrity. The other is that without technical help, Wesley School would not have the curriculum or the results that it has achieved. The message conveyed by *Prime Time* stressed only the human drama involving Lott – the site based decision, the self-imposed accountability.

Another school that purports to follow the Roundtable Principles of site based management and accountability is the Corporate School in Chicago, which was featured in 1991 on *20/20*. The school is funded by several Chicago-based businesses and has a pre-kindergarten, and an all-day, all-year-round schedule. On the program, the principal indicated that if the students don't perform, she gets fired.

In many ways, this school (at the present writing) is not the model of excellence it purports to be. Although it certainly does a better job academically than typical inner-city schools in Chicago, the students are not achieving at "world-class" levels – even though they start as 2-year-olds. The person who directs the Corporate School, Walter Kraus, understands that the performance of the kids may not be what it could be, but he doesn't know how to direct the staff to achieve improved performance or how to identify reliable consultants.

A similar situation exists in Los Angeles, where LEARN has been formed as a coalition of civic leaders and representatives of the community to implement systemic changes that will "enrich the quality of their educational experience and measurably improve their academic growth and achievement."

LEARN is dedicated to: "Transferring decision-making authority to parents, teachers, and principals at the school-site; Holding empowered school-site decision-makers accountable based on school performance measured by a meaningful assessment program."

LEARN, paradoxically, is dedicated to the principle of teacher autonomy.

LEARN's approach assumes that by working with various groups, including Los Angeles Unified School District, it will "arrive at a consensus on its reform agenda from the many diverse constituencies..."

Unfortunately, LEARN will learn too late that consensus in education guarantees failure. It is not as if these "cooperative" practices haven't been tried out before. As part of the National Follow Through project, there were self-sponsored sites. Los Angeles had one; San Diego had one. Self-sponsored sites were supposed to do the site-based thing – identify what the kids' needs are, respond with practices that focus on these needs, operate with a certain amount of autonomy. The plan didn't work. The average performance of Title 1 students was at about the 20th percentile. The self-sponsored sites consistently performed well below this level. In fact, the performance of all the self-sponsored sites was so poor that Follow Through ultimately did away with them. Site-based models failed. Those with strong operating plans worked much better.

It could be argued that one of the reasons the site-based models failed so thoroughly was that they did not have methods of accountability, but it's not obvious that the installation of such accountability is practical. Accountability is premised on the notion that certain performance levels of the kids are **possible**. If the minimum levels are not being reached by anybody, it's not obvious that the desired achievements are possible.

Accountability also assumes that there are measures in place to permit timely identification of problems. For most of the things a staff would collectively decide to do, there are no such measures. Therefore, the school year is something like a tunnel. "Autonomous" teachers and their kids disappear in it at the beginning of the school year. Sometime during the next year, they come out the other end. At that time, the staff may know some of the deficiencies in the kids; however, they may not know what to do about them.

Site-based operations can be effective, but they require the right staff and leaders. A very good principal in Rio Linda, California did it years ago. He started with no assumptions about what worked and what didn't – merely with the blueprint that he would support whatever his teachers wanted to do. They would evaluate the results of

Chapter 11: Give Them the Business

their efforts in a timely manner. If they were not achieving the kind of results they had anticipated, they would change to a new approach immediately. And they would never go back to an approach that had failed. The school, which was the lowest in the district, went through a number of approaches during a two-year period before the staff tried Direct Instruction. Direct Instruction worked. The gains in the site were impressive, with the kids reaching very high achievement levels, well above the 50th percentile.

LEARN's format of teacher autonomy, site-based practices, "accountability," however, is like trying to run a world-class gymnastic training program for young kids by bringing in coaches who have never trained successfully before, and permitting each coach to design a program. A more efficient plan would be to start with people who know how to do it.

The problems of school governance are serious, and unless they are solved, the local efforts — even those that have the potential to work — will be squashed by the bureaucracy. One promising solution is for the Board of Education to contract with outfits other than the local school district. This has already been done in some California cities, such as San Diego, for instance, where the Institute for Effective Education accommodates children who cannot be taught in school (because of behavior problems or serious knowledge-deficit problems). The Institute does an outstanding job. The NASDC funding of "break-the-mold" educational environments is premised on the idea that there will be communities in which the governance plans permit private enterprise to contract with the districts.

The current business-based reforms assume that measurement instruments are important. NASDC also recognizes that "standardized measures" such as those being developed by the Governor's council will not be adequate to assess whether programs are successful. They will have to be supplemented by assessment devices that actually measure what is taught in the different instructional programs. Another side of assessment, however, is that it dictates what teachers teach. Often this dictate is not healthy. In New Jersey, there are quarterly teaching objectives. Some teachers simply use these objectives as their curriculum. They teach the test items so their kids will look good. The assessment instrument has therefore become the curriculum guide.

The same thing will happen with the adoption of National Assessment measures. A percentage of teachers will teach the test items. If the evaluation is based on NCTM standards, the test may include fractions for grade 1 or 2 (given that these grades are tested). Teachers are therefore forced to "teach" about fractions in these grades. That would be unfortunate, particularly if the teachers were using an instructional program that taught fractions carefully in a later grade. The test should not override the curriculum.

Unfortunately, the recurring theme in education is that those who make decisions are not technical experts. Therefore, technical problems are often swallowed by rhetoric about general principles — even in areas like testing. An example comes from Educational Testing Service (ETS).

Educational Testing Service makes up *Reading Objectives* each year. In true democratic form, the *Objectives* are based on the **opinions** of educators, not on the content of the programs that are taught in classrooms. The governing Board sends out a letter to selected educators in an attempt to achieve some sort of "consensus." As the Board put it in its 1989 letter of invitation for opinions: "We recognize that a consensus of reading assessment objectives will be difficult to achieve. However, we wish to involve a broad cross-section of individuals who are concerned about reading in the schools…"

It seems that the Board is starting from the wrong place. If the goal is to determine precisely where the schools are failing or why they are failing, the approach should start with **what the schools are doing**. If the goal is to create new instructional foci, the questionnaire should go to parents, not to educators. The survey approach simply assures that the majority opinions in education will become the major input for the sorting-machine.

For the 1990 assessment of reading, the survey results become translated into familiar rhetoric. According to the *Objectives*, "In particular, efforts were made to integrate new theory and research on the learning and teaching of reading and to reflect innovative approaches to reading assessments developed in Michigan and Illinois as part of their state assessment programs." A footnote following this quote cites a resolution from the International Reading Association: "Resolved that...reading assessments reflect recent advances in the understanding of the reading process...[and that] assessment measures defining reading as a sequence of discrete skills be discouraged." Those are whole-language criteria.

A few pages later in the *Objectives* is rhetoric that contradicts the rhetoric above. "For informational texts, typical items focus on main ideas, author's purpose and related sequences of details..." Wait a minute. These are the skills that were just put down, and they're the same tired items that have been with us from the beginning of achievement testing.

The section that describes how the various items were selected for the 1990 assessment explains that items were evaluated according to concurrence with assessment objectives, content, quality of writing, difficulty, and format. The content was screened for "literary and content richness, development, accuracy, and perceived relevant to students' interests or experiences. While recognizing that much of what students read may conform to less rigorous standards than these, the panel intended that passages included in the assessment be of high quality."

Are you impressed yet? If not, consider how the test items were developed. The development panel used text mapping:

> Text mapping guides item writers in highlighting critical aspects of text. Using text mapping procedures, item writers diagram each passage, producing a graphic organizer that reveals the hierarchical structure of various text elements, depicts relationships among various elements of the text, and classifies distinctions between more and less important elements...Item writers then use the relations depicted within the text maps to generate assessment items that target meaningful aspects of informational passages...The items were written to focus on meaningful rather than trivial aspects of each passage, encouraging readers to think critically about

the questions and reflect back on the passages before arriving at the correct answer.

The *Reading Objectives* might have been more convincing if it didn't include samples. The first sample presented, however, dispels all doubt about the relationship of rhetoric to output. This carefully mapped, absolutely high quality passage is designed for kids in grade four. Consider fourth graders – nine-year-olds – reading this passage and how they would appreciate its relevance to their interests and experience. (Don't skim it. Read it, even though it may hurt.)

Living in an Environment

> Where you live is important. In fact, the survival of all living things depends on where they live. The surroundings of a living thing are called its environment. Your environment includes all the living and nonliving things that affect your life.
>
> Ecosystems – A marsh ecosystem has several types of plants and animals. All of the same type of organisms living in a certain place make up a population. The populations may be large or small. The marsh grass is one population of plants. The heron, crab, and raccoon each belong to different animal populations.
>
> All of the different populations in a given area make up a community. The marsh community includes many kinds of plants, mammals, birds, fish, insects, amphibians, and mollusks. These living things in a community depend on many nonliving things in their environment. Air, moisture, soil, and light are just a few nonliving things that living things need to survive.
>
> A community and its nonliving things are called an ecosystem. An ecosystem can be as large as an ocean or as small as a puddle. A marsh is one example of an ecosystem.
>
> Nonliving Things – Populations that live in the same ecosystem have common needs, such as water and shade. You would not find a water lily growing in a desert. Nor would you find a cactus growing in a pond. These plants would live in ecosystems that fit their needs. The nonliving things in an ecosystem often determine the ecosystem's community, and they can limit the type and size of a community.

Chapter 11: Give Them the Business

Feeding Relationships – The feeding relationships in an ecosystem limit the size of populations. Food relationships begin with plants, since plants use energy from sunlight to produce their own food. For this reason, plants are known as producers.

The food stored in plants is eaten by animals, such as zebras. And these animals are eaten by other animals, such as lions. Therefore, zebras are consumers of plants, and lions are consumers of zebras. A consumer is an organism that feeds on other plants or animals. Predators are animals that hunt, kill, and eat other animals, which are called prey. For example, lions are predators and zebras are prey.

How can these feeding relationships limit the size of different populations? Suppose people kill many lions. With fewer lions to hunt zebras, the zebra population can increase rapidly. The zebras graze more, killing the grasses. With less grass to eat, many zebras may die.

Mode of Reading: Constructs Meaning

1. Which of the following best tells the central purpose of this passage?

    A. Sunlight is the most important factor in an ecosystem.

    B. Living things in an ecosystem depend on each other and on nonliving things.

    C. The size of a population in an ecosystem is important for survival.

    D. Feeding relationships depend on the number of predators in an ecosystem.

2. What is an ecosystem?

    A. All of the living things in an area

    B. All of the nonliving things that a community needs.

    C. The different populations and nonliving things in an area

    D. The nonliving things and water in an area

3. What do the living things in an ecosystem have in common?

    A. They all eat the same food.

    B. They need many of the same nonliving things.

C. They are all similar in size.

D. They are all predators.

4. Why are plants known as producers?

A. Plants provide food for other living things.

B. Plants make their own food.

C. Plants provide oxygen for the ecosystem.

D. Plants are eaten by predators.

Mode of Reading: Extends or Examines Meaning

5. What will happen if too many predators in an ecosystem are killed?

A. The grasses will not be eaten.

B. The oxygen supply will be limited.

C. Producers will not be able to make enough food.

D. The amounts of different kinds of food in the ecosystem will be changed.

What happened to all those splendid criteria about quality of writing, difficulty, and format? This passage would be horrible for kids at any grade level. It is a diarrhetic outflow of words and sentences that shouldn't be. ("The heron, crab and raccoon **each** belong to **different** animal populations." Is that really what the writer is trying to say?) The passage also uses cute language: "The nonliving things in an ecosystem often determine the ecosystem's community…" That sentence just might not ring the "meaning bell" for the fourth grader. Nor would many of the words, starting with **ecosystem**, which is never related to **environment**. Others include **organism, amphibians, mollusks, moisture, prey, predator,** and **limit**.

The passage presents that tired myth about plants: "…plants use energy from sunlight to produce their own food." The most interesting aspect of the passage, however, is not what it does, but how that development team used text mapping. They're probably much better at text mapping than I am, but I made the following map, which seems to show the major relationships and cross-relationships.

Chapter 11: Give Them the Business

Ecosystem - Environment

Nonliving things	limit		living things that form a community	
• Water • Oxygen • CO2 • "Minerals" in Soil • Sunlight	**Feeding relations**	• *producers* • *consumers*	are plants are animals that eat plants or animals	⎫ ⎪ ⎪ Organisms ⎬ in ⎪ different ⎪ populations ⎭
	LIMIT populations	• *plant eaters* • *predators* • *prey*	are animals that eat plants are animals that eat animals are animals eaten by predators	

The overall relationship involves limiting. Nonliving things limit living things. However, there's another limit. Feeding relations limit populations.

Living things are cross-categorized in different ways. All are organisms, and all are organized into different populations that form communities when they are in the same place. The organisms are also ordered according to their feeding relationships, starting with producers (plants) and consumers (animals). The animals are, of course, divided into those that consume plants, those that consume other animals, and those that are consumed by other animals. And all that information – the classifications, the "definitions" (such as they are), the relationships – squeezed into a 500-word passage. The writers of the 1990 *Objectives* assert that "much of what students read may conform to less rigorous standards" than those provided in this assessment. If that's true, I'd really hate to be a nine-year-old.

In any case, we see once more great consistency in how educators approach decision making. They focus primarily on using discourse to sell what they do; however, the fact is that whether they are involved in tests, texts, or practices, technical understanding is lacking.

The business community may learn this lesson in time, but until it does, it will attempt to work cooperatively with people who have never done it, accept their claims that they know how to solve the problems if they have sufficient money or sufficient latitude in decision making, and watch in frustration as plans fail. The enforcement of "accountability" will be difficult if it means firing everybody, but if the staffs are permitted to pursue their own idioms of what is needed to achieve high performance standards, successes will be rare and very expensive. Those who fail will exert great pressure to make failure look like success. And years will pass before the business community learns that the educational decision maker is usually NOT the solution to the problem, but the cause.

CHAPTER 12
HOW SCHOOLS GUARANTEE FAILURE

One of the greatest paradoxes of school districts is that they sometimes undertake projects that require very specific skills. The stance is paradoxical because the districts exist almost exclusively in the world of tabloids and global solutions. Furthermore, the operational theme of districts is typically, "pass it down." Whenever a district is required to implement anything involving instruction or management, some person is identified to direct the implementation. The director of the project, who, typically has no understanding of how to implement, passes the assignment down to an underling who in turn passes it down to someone else. Along the way, some variation of the rules and procedures reach the teachers, who have probably learned that such rules are to be passionately ignored.

Obviously, a district is not well equipped to develop instructional materials. However, they sometimes do it.

Beginning in 1978, we were involved in a series of episodes with a district that made up its own programs. The site was San Diego, which had been a self-sponsored model in Follow Through for ten years. San Diego had performed so poorly (with their third grade kids around the 11th percentile, which means 11th from the bottom out of 100 kids) that the Feds informed San Diego that it would no longer be funded unless it selected from one of two sponsors – the Behavioral Analysis model, or the Direct Instruction model. San Diego selected the latter and we began working in seven of the lowest performing schools in the district.

From the first days of implementation, we had a series of battles with the district, often over conflicts between the way we insisted on running the program and the way the district insisted that it had to be run. For instance, we discovered during the first year that some kids were being pulled out of our classrooms to be "taught" by a school psychologist. We had clearly stipulated in our agreement with San Diego that we would handle "psychological services" for the kids in the program and that these services would be provided within the classroom. A much more serious issue had to do with the Spanish-speaking kids. The district had a bilingual program run by one of the many underling superintendents. The program was a sham, with kids who had spent three or four years in a school not able to produce more than word-salad in English. We had indicated that we would not permit our kids to be involved in the district's "bilingual program," and that we would teach them English as part of the regular-classroom practices. One day, we received a letter from Lisa Sanches, the assistant superintendent, informing us that according to state bilingual regulations and district regulations, kids had to be taught in their native language first (which is what San Diego did in its program). Our plan of teaching kids in English from day one was, according to Sanches, in violation of these regulations.

There it was, in writing and very official looking. But, of course, it was a lie. We called the State Director and the legal council for bilingual programs in Sacramento. Both indicated that no such regulation existed, that the methods for instructing the kids were not specified, except that the instruction should be designed so the kids were able to participate. The district continued to give us static on the issue of bilingual kids. We were required to get "waivers" from parents, but the waivers did not seem to make it from the central office in a timely manner, so we made up our own waivers and had the parents sign them.

The next major episode had to do with the district's attempt to design an instructional program and superimpose it on the Follow Through program. The motivation for this program derived from a complicated set of circumstances. San Diego had lost a desegregation suit. Judge Lorin Welsh recognized that it was not possible to physically desegregate the entire community, and he ordered the implementation of programs that would produce superior educational outcomes for minority kids.

The district responded by designing what it called its Achievement Goals Program (AGP). The reading program that the district used was Ginn, a typical sight-reading program featuring Dick and Jane. The district somehow assumed that they could "bolster" this program with some additional worksheets and make it an exemplary program for minority kids. At the time, one vogue was "mastery learning" programs, which is what San Diego was attempting to create. Judge Welsh expressed concern when he discovered that San Diego planned to start from scratch and do it on their own without using materials that had already been developed. The Deputy Superintendent responded with these opening remarks, "We recognize the magnitude of this extremely complex undertaking. But we make no apologies."

Judge Welsh countered with an observation that Rudolph Flesh listed Ginn as one of the "dismal dozen" publishers of "look-say" approaches.

Judge Welsh commissioned consultants to evaluate the problems and plans in San Diego, and remarkably, he found knowledgeable people. Those who did not meet Welsh's standards received recognition in foot notes in one of his memoranda concerning the desegregation order. For example: "The other consultant, Herbert J. Walberg, reviewed material at his desk in Chicago, made a few telephone calls to personnel in San Diego and sent in a two-page report with a 22-page curriculum vita."

One consultant, Dr. Estes, a superintendent in Atlanta, presented a 14-page report with very astute observations, such as, "The Central Administration appears to believe in, and have confidence in the expertise and abilities of currently assigned teachers and local site administrators...However, it is suggested that some type of assessment devices and mechanisms be instituted and utilized to verify or refute this belief."

Indeed, the district had no plans to monitor the implementation or to concern itself with accountability. Judge Welsh was remarkably incisive at identifying the administrative problems in San Diego. He wrote, "If there are a dozen curricular offerings in a school, there may be a dozen persons responsible for their implementation. Successful solutions to common problems in one school will be unknown to those at other schools. There appears to be no solid coordination among programs."

And Judge Welsh observed that the district was not always a paragon of truthfulness. "The credibility of the District with this Court has deteriorated because of lack of candor. Statistical analyses in District evaluations are changed from report to report in order to exaggerate claimed successes and minimize failures."

The judge ordered the district to work out plans so that there was monitoring and accountability. That's where our program became involved in the scheme. We had those components. Our program had a project manager who worked with three district "resource teachers" who served as monitors and trainers. They were wonderful young women – smart, reliable, and completely dedicated to helping kids and teachers. We had schedules, daily criteria, feedback procedures, and strict rules for accountability. The project manager was responsible for the implementation – period. If something threatened the implementation and the project manager was unable to deal with it, she bumped it up to me. Each resource teacher had clearly defined responsibilities. The teachers in the classroom were responsible for achieving minimum reasonable performance gains with kids (measured on a bi-weekly basis through performance tests). All in-service training was determined by common problems among teachers.

Apparently, the district felt that if it took the Achievement Goals Program and overlaid it with our operational system, it would be as effective as our project. I found out about this plan when I was invited to a meeting of many superintendents. Their proposal was for AGP to merge with Direct Instruction, and we would use AGP in our Follow Through program.

Naturally, my answer was "No." I tried to explain that you couldn't make Dick and Jane into a successful reading program by dealing with the visible things that the administration had observed. I also tried to explain that you don't make an effective instructional program the way the district was going about it. They became quite irritated – more accurately, red-necked mad. They argued about the virtues of their approach. Finally, I pointed out that the only reason we were in that district was because they failed and that they were not actually instructional experts. I told them that so long as the Feds supported us, we would run Follow Through using the same practices and programs that had succeeded in other sites.

I'm sure the administrators thought that I was just being a smart ass, and that they weren't being arrogant. But their arrogance was amazing. They knew nothing about instruction; yet they had not the slightest doubts about whether they had discovered what really makes an implementation succeed and whether they could do it as well as or better than anybody else.

The district went ahead with the AGP development. It gave teachers leave to make up worksheets and supplemental material — hundreds and hundreds of worksheets for each level of the program. And the district implemented a "monitoring and accountability" plan that was superficially fashioned after that of Follow Through, except for one small detail: The people in Follow Through were carefully trained for their positions.

The project manager could be held responsible for the implementation of a site because she had demonstrated that she was a superstar teacher and a superstar trainer before she ever became a project manager. She didn't just step in off the street.

The resource teachers had been there during San Diego's self-sponsored reign. They later became superstars because they were trained — first in teaching; then in supervising. Granted, they were as smart as any people we had ever worked with, but they didn't just happen. Nor did any other detail of the program just happen. If anybody in the district had bothered to study what's involved in refining these details, they would have understood that it's highly improbable for a group of superintendents sitting at a conference table either to observe critical details or to design them.

AGP forged ahead. For the school year of 1980-81, the district presented the board with a comparison of AGP and *DISTAR* (or Follow Through). The report, in the tradition of "candor" that Judge Welsh had observed, was a farce. It was provided by Robert Smith of USC. The Follow Through schools were the lowest in the district. Smith did not compare the scores of current Follow Through with those of the self-sponsored era. Instead, he simply presented the scores of the kids before and after Grade 1 and concluded, "*DISTAR* and AGP have roughly comparable populations in terms of measured reading achievement at the beginning of Grade 1 and both programs evidence comparable changes during Grade 1." The summary indicated that 64 percent of the *DISTAR* kids were at or above grade level in reading at the beginning of grade 1, and at the end of the grade, 57.9 percent were at or above average median performance. AGP had similar figures.

The first question you might ask is, "Why were kids in San Diego's lowest schools performing at such a high level when they entered first grade?" The Follow Through kids had gone through kindergarten, and the kindergarten they went through had taught academic skills. We gave kids achievement tests when they **entered kindergarten**. The average entering kid at some of the schools we worked in scored at the second percentile (second from the bottom in a population of 100 kids). At the end of kindergarten, they were obviously smarter than average. But to compare these kids with AGP kids who "naturally" enter first grade performing above grade level is to present a very distorted comparison.

Smith's report had other distortions. One had to do with the kids who had finished grade 2. These kids were not performing as well as the grade 1 kids. Furthermore, their performance upon entering grade 2 was lower than the performance of kids at the end of grade 1. Smith couldn't solve this conundrum. He observed, "*DISTAR* and AGP have differing populations in terms of measured reading achievement at the beginning of grade 2. This is a somewhat surprising find since grade 2 pretests are grade 1 posttests."

What Smith failed to understand is that the first year of an implementation is a shakedown year, particularly in a place where teachers have a history of not teaching effectively. The kids who completed grade 2 had been in kindergarten during the first year the project was implemented. Their performance was significantly lower than that of later waves of kids at the end of K, at the end of 1, and at the end of 2. The second wave of kids who completed grade 1 received much better instruction in K, so they were higher at the end of kindergarten and at the end of grade 1. Therefore, the latest wave of kids finishing grade 1 had much higher scores than the kids who had begun grade 2 the year before.

Smith's report went into the cost of implementing AGP and *DISTAR*. His figures showed clearly that the cost of implementing *DISTAR* was greater than that of AGP. The conclusions, although unstated, were obvious. AGP does as well as *DISTAR* with "comparable" populations. AGP costs less. Therefore…

Interestingly enough, during the following school year, San Diego's AGP program contradicted its alleged inexpensiveness by going over projected budget. It didn't exceed expectations by a few dollars – the cost of simply reproducing material exceeded the anticipated cost of the entire project by more than $1 million. AGP slowly faded into that graveyard of abortive reforms.

These episodes with San Diego were painful. For a project to succeed with kids who enter school performing far below norms, everything must be in place, and everything must be done right. If one first-grade teacher screws up, the kids will show an enormous drop in performance. It's not as if these kids would pick it up anyhow. They'll drop down to where they would have been expected to perform without the program. To guarantee that all the details are in place requires an incredible amount of work even if there are no administrative obstacles blocking what you're trying to do. You have to train teachers in practices that are foreign to them. You have to support them, help them, and in some cases, try to remove them from the project. In the meantime, their kids may not receive the kind of teaching that's required for a high-quality implementation. At the end of the year, these kids are behind. Even if the teacher in the next grade is excellent, there is little she can do to compensate for the loss that occurred during the preceding year.

We had worked on these details, and we had shaped San Diego into a very good implementation, despite interference from the district. A lot of people put their souls in that project, but in the end, it didn't seem to make much difference. One of the last interactions we had with the district was over their proposed "Rainbow Project," designed for kids in grades four through six. It was to be modeled after Follow Through and run by the district, which now had a new superintendent. I wrote him and tried to explain some of the pitfalls and the need for outside people to help train those who were to supervise the program. The

Chapter 12: How Schools Guarantee Failure

response I received was reminiscent of the Deputy Superintendent's optimistic position about designing AGP. The superintendent referred to the stellar evaluations that I had given our resource teachers and assured me that the district had other talented resource teachers who could achieve the same kind of results with the "Rainbow Project."

The "Rainbow Project" turned out to be a complete bust — a big-time failure.

San Diego shows some of the ways that schools guarantee failure. The first is for administrators to assume that they know how to do something they have never done. The second is to superficially copy something that works. The third is to lie or distort to protect administrators. All of the above is possible because in the final analysis, administrators are not on the same side of the fence as the kids. The problem results partly from the administration's knowledge deficit about instruction and partly from a structural problem. When kids fail, the kids' lives are affected greatly; however, the lives of administrators who designed the failures are not affected.

Interestingly enough, there are people who seem to understand what should be done. Judge Welsh provided a refreshing contrast with the administration. He knew nothing about education when he was assigned to the case, but he found out what works; he found people who could produce informed analyses; and he identified the structural problems with the administration.

Unfortunately, school districts don't typically reason the same way Judge Welsh did. Once I was invited to be a last-minute presenter at a conference in Seattle. The topic was the disadvantaged and quality education. The reason for my last-minute invitation was that the Seattle evaluation department had discovered that a disproportionately high percentage of black kids in the district's gifted program had gone through a Direct-Instruction preschool-kindergarten (CAMPI). My talk in Seattle basically outlined the different details that had to be controlled to achieve an over all successful implementation (the kind of controls that had been in place in CAMPI). I outlined what would have to be done to achieve such quality controls in other grades. When I finished talking, one of the administrators asked, "But isn't there an easier way? That's so much work and attention to details."

I told her that so far as I knew, there is no simple way. I was tempted to say something like, "Don't you think that if there were an easier way, somebody would have long since discovered it? After all, every magical, easy, and global approach that could penetrate the collective educational imagination has been tried out ad nauseam."

Another way that schools guarantee failure is by misapplying democracy to create mandates by committee. We saw an example of this approach with the voting approach used by the National Assessment Governing Board, which polled educators about their priorities for reading objectives. School districts and State Departments of instruction often use this technique.

An example was a questionnaire sent in 1989 to all teachers and staff in Montana by the Office of Public Instruction (OPI). The document opened with one of those newsletter hypes that seem to be popular in education:

> These are exciting times to be involved in education. It is a time to look forward. A time to develop programs which will enable our students to step into the 21st Century. The Office of Public Instruction is in the process of drafting curriculum guides. These guides could be used as models by districts in their curriculum planning. Your input is needed. This is an opportunity for you to have a voice in shaping reading curriculum...

The questionnaire consisted of these items:

1. Briefly describe your philosophy of reading.

2. What are your recommendations for an ideal program based on the latest research findings?

3. What in your estimation are some of the issues in reading facing us today?

4. What kind of technical assistance would you like from the reading specialist at OPI?

5. If a state reading task force is formed, would you be willing to serve?

I'm not sure how the state planned to used the information provided by these responses, and I'm less sure that the information has any but demographic significance. What if 81 percent of the respondents indicated that their philosophy of reading was whole language? Would that percentage validate whole language, or would it simply (a) provide an excuse for the OPI when the approach proves to be a bust, and (b) imply that the percentage of people in Montana who are knowledgeable about instruction is very small?

Item 2 of the questionnaire calls for the respondent's recommendations for an ideal program based on the latest research findings. What does the average teacher know about the latest research findings? What percentage of teachers read "research" studies or even understand the difference between research on instruction and research that simply shows what kids tend to do?

And who do you think would want to sign up for a task force? Good teachers often avoid these committees because they know that most of the people in the group will be very naive and will view any dissenters as trouble makers. In the end, the good teacher's suggestions will be ignored.

I wrote a response to the OPI items, at the request of a dentist in Montana (Dean Anderson) who had been concerned about the whole-language movement in the state. My response ended with the basic question of what the OPI expected to learn from the questionnaire. Here's my somewhat understated closing paragraph:

> You should be concerned with people who can answer your questions, because they know how to do it. To treat the game as a microcosm of democracy, or a consensus game, will yield more of what you already have, suggestions based on no knowledge of effective solutions. There are tons of studies that show how naive the general teacher, the average supervisor and the typical principal are about instructional materials, diagnosis and remedies. Your goal should be to upgrade these folks, not to solicit their advice. Shame on you.

The bottom line is the rather ugly fact that the most serious problems of education could be obviated if it were somehow possible to work with the teachers and kids without first having to pass through a typical school district's administration. That administration guarantees failure of programs by its very existence. The administration does not facilitate; it obstructs. It does not learn; it is convinced that it is an expert in instructional matters and therefore "tells"; it does not treat the performance of kids as the yardstick for what it does and gear what it does to the data on kid performance. It references its performance to slogans and the acceptance of peers who parrot the same slogans. It does not use quality-control measures that identify problems; it uses rhetoric to make its failures look like successes.

So long as school districts are permitted to construct obstacles through their guidelines and their mandated practices, there will be no excellence in education. An occasional exemplary program will spring up, but it will die, and the administration will later have no memory of its life or its death, because the people who compose this administration will be new people with new and rich ideas, based on the latest opinions about how kids learn.

CHAPTER 13
HOW TEACHER COLLEGES GUARANTEE FAILURE

People in education are products of their education. Their deficiencies, their sense of priorities, and their orientation to knowledge are fashioned by what they've experienced and what their mentors have written and said. While the engrams of college training are pronounced on teachers, their deficiencies can be corrected because teachers are actually in contact with instruction, kids, and the concrete facts of education. Many of their philosophical beliefs are vulnerable when they come into contact with these realities. I've worked with a lot of teachers who have started out with disguised sorting-machine philosophies, such as, "I want kids to be themselves and choose what they want to learn. I don't want to manipulate them." I've seen some of these teachers go into inner-city classrooms of kids, with dreams of how the kids will learn and grow, only to discover how kids actually respond when given the license to "negotiate" on the basis of their interests and personal style. I've seen kids transform teachers' dreams into nightmares and transform the teachers into suspicious, bitter individuals.

Not all teachers become bitter. Many adapt by learning techniques for keeping the classroom orderly and setting goals far more modest than those they had when they came out of college. Some persist in trying to find ways to reach and teach kids. And a few of them find methods that work. Occasionally, they do it on their own, but in most cases, they learn from a model – somebody who shows them how to do it. Unfortunately, most who have the right attitude about their role in serving the kids are never exposed to effective models. Usually, they are insulated from such exposure by the school administration, which all but assures that what they hear about effective methods is distorted.

Value systems play a role in these distortions. The appeal to a teacher is liberal. The teacher is billed as an agent of change who is made privy to new insights that derive from the research of other liberals.

Those who promote opposing approaches, such as phonics, are advertised as being somewhere to the right of Mussolini in their educational orientation. Those who promote the application of "behavioral methods" are declared mechanists, manipulators, and people who would challenge the natural order of things. Anybody advocating "skill" instruction is a reactionary, a primate who has apparently been absent from the educational scene for thirty years. Direct Instruction is seen as a "grunt and spit" approach to the delicate business of nurturing children.

Arguments provided by the establishment are effective for one simple reason: the establishment consists of many, many people. When they raise their voice in a choral recitation of the established arguments, people like you and the typical teacher believe them. The slogans that support favored approaches bristle with moral righteousness and give the impression that the approach or process has an exclusive franchise on morality.

While beliefs of teachers are potentially vulnerable because of their exposure to "hands on" evidence about kids, the prejudices of administrators are more resistant because decision makers live in the world of rhetoric.

Graduate training shapes prejudices that administrators carry with them. For instance, an administrator preparing for a position in secondary schools may be required to take some courses that are supposed to address issues of curricula. Possibly, they must take a course titled "Secondary School Curriculum," or something similar. The course title suggests curricular issues that are important for the teacher or administrator, such as the high school kid who is far behind where he should be — the kid who is turned off and who must sit through courses that present material so far from his understanding that the teacher's explanation becomes noise. What do you do with that kid? How do you design curricular programs that don't continue to punish him? How do you go about fixing him up, modifying the standard curricula for his particular "needs," and restoring his crippled image of himself?

Another issue is the "sequencing" of what kids learn in high school and some of the current abuses. For instance, there's a debate among high-school biology teachers about how much time, if any, should be spent on teaching facts of basic chemistry before launching into cell biology. Consider that most high-school biology students have not studied any chemistry, and may not know what a chemical reaction is; however, they study biology, much of which is nothing but chemistry, and very complicated chemistry. The consensus seems to be to assign the kids a chapter that presents some information on chemistry, launch into biology, and when the kids get helplessly stuck over trying to understand what is happening during cell respiration, present more information "as needed." Teachers who support this consensus believe that because the students will study chemistry the following year, they'll be able to synthesize what they learned in biology with the facts about chemistry. Of course, this plan is insane. It's very difficult to synthesize gibberish.

A related issue in high school curricula is the "textbook," which is probably a misnomer. For many subjects, the "textbook" is not designed to teach the student in a progressive and systematic way. It is a reference book, with the earlier chapters written with no concern about the fact that kids have not yet read the later chapters. The average high-school text in biology, for example, introduces about three times the number of new, unfamiliar words that would be recommended for the first year of learning a foreign language. What makes this figure even more astonishing is that the concepts behind these words are new (unlike the foreign language that presents new words for familiar ideas).

For instance, on page 106 of Holt's *Biology* text, the following words are introduced for the first time:

> Chromatin network, nucleoli, centrosome, centroiols, DNA, mitosis, prophase, astral rays, aster, chromosomes, chomatids, centromere, spindle, pole, metaphase, anaphase, and telophase.

A reasonable topic for discussion of secondary-school curricula would be whether these texts are reasonable, whether they are consistent with new theories about the ways kids learn, or whether they are designed to promote the use of pain killers and other forms of escape. Similar problems exist in math and English.

Another issue is whether testing in the high schools should be cumulative, that is, a progressive series of tests that assess the basic material as well as the most recently introduced concepts and facts. This topic has implications for textbook design and for grade-level requirements.

Of course, the issue of kid performance is paramount, and since curricula are at the heart of the problem, the administrator-to-be should be acquainted both with the causes of student-performance problems and effective solutions – that is, solutions that have been demonstrated to work.

Hundreds of side issues flank these central issues, such as the caste system our current curricula are promoting and the projection that participation in the future will be circumscribed by knowledge that only a few will have. How many of these issues would be covered in the course "Secondary School Curriculum"? Probably none. They are simply not the kinds of issues that are considered appropriate by most educators. They are not "broad" enough or "historical" enough. They do not lend themselves to either the type of theory or level of rhetoric that is apparently deemed appropriate for graduate work. The kid who fails might be discussed, but in the context of sociological and psychological constructs. The sequence of what is presented in schools might be mentioned, but as part of a much broader discussion about the role of the school in interfacing with society.

A course on secondary school curriculum, which had been offered at the University of Oregon, hammered home a few "general principles" to the students. The first is that "scientific" approaches to instruction or to school management are misguided. A corollary is that means-end reasoning is not appropriate for dealing with curricular issues. The third is that the teachers – like the students in the course – should be equipped with general principles, not with specific skills. The reading list for the course thoroughly develops these prejudices.

One selection written by Kliebard, "The Rise of Scientific Curriculum Making and Its Aftermath," points out the preposterous attempts of a pair of obscure characters (Bobbitt and Charters) in the early 20th century to apply scientific principles (more accurately those deriving largely from time-and-motion studies) to curricula. Kliebard makes some valid points. He points out that the establishment is very presumptuous in believing that it knows how to solve far-flung problems:

> Hence, if curriculum makers do not temper the question of what is the most important to know with the question of what schools can accomplish, their claims for programs designed to reduce crime, improve human relations, prevent drunken driving, ensure economic independence, or remove sex inhibitions are unreliable.

In the end, however, Kliebard's arguments are hollow. He suggests that current attempts to design curricula "scientifically" are an extension of the efforts of Bobbitt and Charters, that attempts to train teachers scientifically have flopped, and that teacher training is largely the domain of the philosophical, not the scientific. As Kliebard puts it:

> The process of educating a teacher to conduct himself or herself wisely and judiciously in the classroom is not, as current programs of teacher training so often imply, a process of first anticipating the particular situations that will arise in the classroom and then directing the teachers to conduct themselves in a particular way relative to these specific situations. Rather, teacher education can involve the examination, analysis and adaptation of some broad principles which at some unknown point in the future and in some unanticipated circumstances may provide a guide to keen judgment and wise action.

I know of very few teacher-training or administration-training programs that do not merchandise the "general principles" and decry the specific, the overt, and the data based. So Kliebard is clearly playing to the home fans. Also, he's wrong. We have done studies on teacher performance in which the kids' performance at the end of the year correlates very highly (about 90 percent) with specific teacher behaviors measured **mid-year**. So there are very strong arguments for careful and scientific teacher-training programs.

More pernicious is Kliebard's suggestion that teachers will benefit from broad principles that will come into play in some unanticipated way and that will lead to keen judgment. My guess would be that a "general principle" that has not been practiced repeatedly in "anticipated" situations will produce a hugs-and-kisses outcome in an unanticipated situation as frequently as the seven-year locust appears. This is sorting-machine rhetoric, and it is perfectly inappropriate for the student who may later be charged with training teachers. The general principle is a very handy device for administrators because in most cases, it's all they have.

Another reading for "Secondary School Curriculum" is written by a philosopher, Richard Peters. The Title: "Must an Educator Have an Aim? The answer would seem to be: Let's damn well hope so. We would hate to see that guy out there doing things that are apparently unrelated to any purpose.

Peters' argument is a little complicated because he doesn't seem to answer the question. His position is that different people could accept the same "goal" or "aim" and use very different methods for reaching this goal. Some would use authority and possibly even brutality, while others (liberals and progressives) would adopt a more sensitive approach. Peters' point seems to be that "there is a quality of life embedded in the activities which constitute education." Self-realization (a goal) "can be explicated only by reference to such activities." According to Peters, decisions about activities involve values; however, "…the model of means to ends is not remotely applicable to the transaction that is taking place."

From the standpoint of logic, Peters' hasn't done anything but displace "goals" from global ones (self-realization) to lesser ones (activities). Both, however, take precisely the same form because both are governed by values:

> So you could express either one in this manner:
>> We should do things that promote X.
>>
>> A particular practice promotes X.
>>
>> Therefore, we should use that practice.

Without using some version of this form, Peters' educator would be unable to perform any action related to a value, because there would be no possible relationship between what he does and his "value."

His values would just apparently build up in his head until they exploded. Given that Peters' educator designs or adopts activities, the educator prima-facie had goals. I suppose it could be argued that Peters' educator simply operates in a random way with no connection between behaviors and values, but that possibility would seriously weaken Peters' suggestion that his educator is sensitive and has a critical mind.

So Peters does not demonstrate in any way that means-ends reasoning is inappropriate, or that goals or aims are any different from the "goals" that are used in the selection of activities. At best, he shows that global goals don't tell it all and that process goals are needed. But who doesn't know this? Let's say we want to teach kids to read better, so we'll starve them until they become better readers. I don't think too many people would buy into this formula even if recent research about how children learned showed that the practice worked.

Aside from the deficiencies in Peters' argument, why was it presented in a course on Secondary Curriculum? Possibly, it is supposed to convey the idea that if you're sensitive and if you deal in largely unspecified instincts, you'll be wise and make decisions that show your understanding of Peters' slogan: "Life must be for the sake of education, not education for life."

One of the readings presented in the course is actually pretty good: "Determinants of Curriculum Change and Stability, 1870-1970," by Larry Cuban. His main point is that while many decisions are made about curricula, these decisions often fail to have the intended effect in the classroom. Cuban observes the basic problem: "Without much basic understanding of the technology of teaching, no solid linkage can be made between what is done and what happens." Cuban also acknowledges the fruitless search for meaning illustrated by educational trends. "The educational past is littered with the debris of innumerable curricular changes that embarrassed school practitioners only to disappear or leave a slight residue." However, these trends don't often give us a good understanding of what occurs in the classroom. As Cuban puts it, studies that actually observed what went on in classrooms found remarkable stability. The observers of one study, "expected to find those highly publicized innovations in content, classroom organization, and instruction..." The observers visited 150 primary grade classrooms in 13 states. But they didn't find, "individualized instruction, team-teaching, ungraded classrooms, inquiry learning, new materials and equipment, and a host of other changes spurred by outside and inside forces." Instead, they found the teacher-dominated classroom. The researchers concluded, "Many of the changes we have believed to be taking place in schooling have not been getting into the classrooms."

Teachers behave pretty much the same way in these classrooms. "Teachers do the asking for the most part and what they ask requires low-level recall and comprehension from students."

Cuban's conclusion is sensible, "...we need far more reliable information about, for example, how teachers teach, deal with children, relate to time and space, cope with unpredictability and uncertainty, and seek satisfaction within the school and classroom."

He closes with this note about research. "There is no need for a long research agenda. Policy makers need a short, simple one that drives people into schools and classrooms to see and learn what are the limits of stability and change. Now they do not know. Until they do, solutions and answers will wander aimlessly in search of problems and questions." Yea, Cuban.

Cuban's position would serve as a good cornerstone for a course designed to teach future policy makers some foundation facts about their business and the discrepancy between rhetoric and practice in education. But the next step would be to address those problems that are specific to secondary-school curriculum. However, the Cuban selection apparently was not included in the readings because of its cornerstone potential, but because it presented the conclusion that there isn't much we know, a theme that is developed methodically by the other readings.

One article, by William Pinar, "The Reconceptualization of Curriculum Studies," presents a historical and sociological view of curriculum and draws a cute little "eclectic" conclusion. After observing that curricularists are often intolerant of others who do not share their orientation, Pinar writes:

I am convinced that this intolerance among curricularists for work differing from one's own must be suspended to some extent if significant intellectual movement in the field is to occur. Becoming open to another genre of work does not mean loss of one's capacity for critical reflection. Nor does it mean, necessarily, loss of intellectual identity. One may remain a traditionalist while sympathetically studying the work of a reconceptualist. One's own point of view may well be enriched.

Nice try, Bill.

When it is possible to help kids who are now failing and when the obstacles to helping them are philosophical beliefs based on superstition, tradition, and dreams (like Bill's) that are presented as serious suggestions, it's very difficult to be tolerant. Tolerance implies suspending a host of moral beliefs, such as the notion that our nation ostensibly is dedicated to equality, the idea that the educational community is supposed to do the best possible job with the cherished possessions of parents who are entrusted to the schools, and the conviction that we are not supposed to be dominated by beliefs like might makes right, which is the essence of the establishment's operational philosophy and emphasis on consensus.

The rest of the course presents more of the same, different positions, often cloaked in political and sociological jargon that does little to clarify the issues. An article by Apple, "The Hidden Curriculum and the Nature of Conflict," concludes that the teaching of science and other subjects does not reveal the conflict that occurs in these fields. Apple's position could probably be summarized in a short paragraph if the sociological and quasi-philosophical issues were scratched. Apple believes that kids who study science are being short changed because they don't learn about conflict. Or, as Apple puts it, "…with this understanding of the social milieu in which curricularists operate, there must also be a continual attempt to bring to a conscious level those hidden epistemological and ideological assumptions that help to structure the decisions they make and the environments they design… These fundamental assumptions can have a significant impact on the hidden curriculum in which students tacitly dwell."

Chapter 13: How Teacher Colleges Guarantee Failure

So somebody should come out with a program that deals with the dialectic of social change in science curriculum. With Apple's course, students learn that something they don't understand (science) is the subject of conflict.

The course on Secondary School Curriculum is generally designed to put down the notion that teaching is a technology and to promote the great myth that the teacher is a sensitive guide who possesses all those positive qualities that are assumed by the establishment. The cornerstone of the course is a book titled, *The Educational Imagination*, by Elliot Eisner. In the tradition of the other readings, it presents essays on different topics that obfuscate the obvious and deface the necessary. One chapter, "On the Art of Teaching," suggests that the technological approach to "instruction" is a rather low-level and misguided pursuit based on an industrial model.

Eisner indicates that any systematic attempts to design curricula or training came straight from the automobile assembly line. Naturally he takes issue with the process of: identifying goals, then "subdividing them into units, and casting them into operational forms," and of taking the next steps of creating "procedures known to be instrumental to the achievement of these goals," and installing a monitoring system "to control the performance patterns of teachers, who, in turn, can control the performance of students."

What's wrong with this plan? Eisner suggests that it is greatly misguided. "The failure to distinguish between education and training, between the school and the factory, between the algorithms and heuristics of teaching accounts for the simplistic nostrums that are promulgated as ways of improving education."

The rhetoric says it all. The good guys educate; the bad guys train. The good guys recognize the institution as the school; the bad guys think of it as a factory. The good guys present stimulating heuristics; the bad guys, low-level algorithms. One minor problem: All the positive findings that compensatory education works, that teachers can be trained to be effective diagnosticians and presenters, and that schools can be managed in a way that dramatically improves kid performance have come from the bad guys, not the good guys.

Furthermore, the insinuation that the factory and school have nothing in common, although a very popular belief in traditional education, is not all that valid, particularly with respect to "operational plans."

The assembly line is progressive, which means that pieces come together to create more complex forms. That's what happens in instruction. Simple parts (skills and concepts) are combined to form more complicated units (applications that cut across various previously taught skills).

The assembly line is governed by the notion of efficiency. The pieces that come together should be on time, not so late that assembly of more complex units is impossible. So it is with the schools. Things are supposed to be taught in a timely fashion. For example, all kids should be taught basic decoding skills by the end of the first grade so they can take the next steps.

The assembly line is based on the idea of quality control. The ideal goal is to produce no damaged merchandise. This goal would be an excellent one for the schools to adopt.

The assembly line has methods for measuring quality. Typically, inspectors examine sampled products at different stations along the assembly line to assure that there are no screw-ups. The inspection stations are positioned so they can identify problems early (not after the entire product has been assembled). Off hand, it's difficult to understand why the schools don't adopt this practice. It certainly would provide the administrator with current information about the performance of kids and would alert the administrator to problems of damaged merchandise.

The assembly line anticipates problems and has "back-up" plans. The scheduling is (ideally) safe enough so that if one machine on the line breaks down and the line must be shut down, a back-up plan may be put into effect (both for completing the product on time and for redirecting the workers on the line). This part of the analogy has to do with the "scheduling" of what is taught in schools. The schedules should be designed to anticipate a percentage of "unpredicted" problems.

Naturally, the nature of the product and the job in the factory are quite different from those of the classroom. The teacher works with living kids, not with inanimate objects. But the structure of the ideal (not the sweat shop and not the poorly designed educational delivery system) is pretty much the same. The worker on the line must make basic quality control decisions. If a machine is screwing up or if there is a problem with the materials that are available, she would call the foreman, right now. So it should be with the quality-control aspects of instruction. Teachers should know when to call for help, and help should be available, right now.

And what seems to be wrong with the model of planning and developing systems "to control the performance patterns of teachers, who, in turn, can control the performance of students"? Certainly the process can be abused, just as a knucklehead engineer can build a bridge that falls down. But what are the alternatives; the sensitive teacher who somehow knows how to do wonderful things with kids? If that's the plan, the system had better hire at least 10 teachers for every one the schools hope to keep.

Eisner thinks that the missing ingredient is intention. Intention is what drives the teacher's fluid, responsive decisions. These intentions may be so elusive that they may not be capable of expression in our language. Eisner asks, "Is it necessary that the aspiration one seeks be statable in discursive language?" I certainly hope so. Consider the downside of the inexpressible "intention." You walk into the classroom during the time the teacher is supposed to be teaching reading and the kids are finger painting. You ask the teacher what she is doing. And the teacher points to her head and says something like, "I can't put it into words. It's an intuition, a feeling. But I know that the children need more finger painting and less reading."

Actually, the teacher has intentions if the teacher has accepted the responsibility for teaching a particular class in a particular setting and if there are goals or objectives that she accepts as part of her responsibilities.

We're not really very interested in freelance intentions, or intentions that are counter to these performance goals.

The general impression left by the course, "Secondary School Curriculum," is the same as that forged by most of the other courses.

Planning and trying to work out standardized procedures is viewed as mechanistic and restrictive. The teacher is viewed as sensitive, knowledgeable, and bursting with intentions, even those that can't be expressed in words. The model of "systematic" teaching is labeled as "factory" approach, while the global, individualistic positions provided by the "essayists" are enlightened.

The typical products of such training (or "education") programs are handicapped and often dangerous administrators. For them it is not arrogant to eschew data because data is the product of the bad guys.

Reform proposals normally flirt with teacher training, but far less frequently do they deal with administrator training. Granted, most colleges of education do a terrible job of training teachers. The problems are largely caused by the "philosophy" of the institution, which is the same philosophy that is bestowed upon those studying to be administrators. Colleges also have serious problems because of their governance structure and the tenure system. With tenure, unproductive faculty are permanent fixtures. The common governance structure of the department often assures that good people will probably not be hired, because ratification of new faculty normally requires a vote of current faculty. So the department frequently represents a self-perpetuating problem.

Reforming the education of administrators, however, would seem to be a very immediate and important goal. The notion of site-based management or school decision making assumes that there is an instructional leader in the school. In fact, the principal typically spends a very small percentage of available time (around ten percent) on instructional matters, typically does not establish curricular or instructional goals, and typically has a healthy respect for "teacher autonomy" because the teachers intimidate most principals. The principal's major function is that of being a conservative agent who vetoes unwanted change but is usually incapable of being an effective agent of change because the principal has no particular skills in the areas of teaching or training teachers.

At the University of Oregon, we have a graduate training program that turns out Ph.D.s who don't quite fit the roles called for by the current system. Instead of training these graduate students in the typical sequence of administration courses, we train them to be teacher trainers. They must first be proficient at teaching. What they learn about training teachers provides immediate contradictions to most of the slogans quoted in this chapter. They observe, in painful detail, the growth of good teachers. They see the problems some teachers have in doing something as seemingly obvious as applying procedures that have been adequately learned for teaching one subject to teaching another subject. (If the teachers are trained in procedures for beginning reading, they often have serious problems using the same procedures when they teach beginning arithmetic, or beginning language.) The trainers see what is actually involved in "programming" a teacher so that she has astute decision-making skills about what students need and has the fluid delivery that Eisner sees as the product of philosophy. They observe just how contraintuitive effective practices are for teachers.

The idiom of teacher training that is generally espoused by the "informed" public is based on the proposal by Robert Hutchins that a good liberal arts background is all that is really needed to prepare the teacher. Unfortunately, Hutchins based this conclusion on observations of teacher-training practices that were peppered with casuistry. Effective practices thoroughly refute the notion that the good intentioned and well educated are prepared to be effective teachers.

Training teachers takes time. Training effective trainers takes even more time. It requires a competent staff, ongoing practice, and lots of feedback.

We implemented the Leadership Ph.D. program at the University of Oregon to train trainers because we felt that the only way school districts would be able to pull themselves out of their mire of incompetence is through intelligent decisions about how to teach kids effectively and how to train teachers effectively. School decision making should be dominated by technical experts who would be able to provide information about what it actually required to implement, why some plans are naive, which alternatives make sense, and how to set up and operate a quality control system.

Ironically, there is no position for such people in the typical district. It's possible for them to get a position with a title like Elementary

Supervisor, but the position is hollow. The Elementary Supervisor has questionable authority. She couldn't give an assignment to a principal or a teacher. She couldn't establish monitoring practices or other quality-control details. Instead, she goes from meeting to meeting, from school to school and functions as something between a counselor, a cheerleader, and a company representative.

In summary, the teacher colleges contribute most greatly to ongoing failure of schools by training administrators who lack fundamental knowledge of what can be done with kids and who consequently lack moral commitment to prevent academic child abuse. They don't recognize abuse because they lack technical skill. They often boast about being eclectic, but for the traditionalist, eclecticism means simply having a head full of contradictory notions that are not viewed as being contradictory.

Administrators with this orientation routinely remove effective instructional programs, sometimes on the grounds that even though the outcomes are good, the "process" is not consistent with their philosophy. They do not view the child being educated as a product; therefore, they do not consider quality-control as an issue. Where hard work and intensive instruction are needed, they see only the need for "opportunity" and the natural creativity of children. They make stupid decisions that hurt children, and they don't even know that the decisions are stupid.

CHAPTER 14
SYSTEMIC CHANGE

The current system cannot work because too many aspects of it are out of phase with what is required for our kids to achieve "world class" standards. Current policies and practices are based on the sorting-machine. An effective system would be strictly referenced to the children. Effective reform cannot target a single aspect of the system but must be characterized by systemic change, a new focus and orchestration of policy around the kids, their problems, and their performance. Major policies and practices must address instruction and must be justifiable in terms of facilitating teaching of kids or of preventing academic child abuse.

The effective system would play two main games. The first is that of carefully installing practices and programs that have data to support the belief that they'll work well. The second game is to devise a quality-control system within the system that is capable of quickly identifying, in great detail, where the system is faltering – with specific children, specific classrooms, specific skills – and point out specific discrepancies between what had been projected and what is observed.

All components and practices within the district would be designed to support these major games. The details of the system and necessary policy are implied by starting with the more general issues of quality-control – for instance, with the need for **assessment**.

1. Documenting problems or success with individual students requires current and accurate information about student performance. Therefore, there must be an assessment procedure that provides accurate and timely assessments of each child. More frequent assessments would be provided in the primary grades (once every 1-3 weeks) and less frequent ones in high school (once every 4-8 weeks). The assessments would not be a "report card," but specific information on how well each student is learning what the teacher is teaching. The assessments would ideally not require a lot of time to administer,

score, or evaluate. Their use would be primarily to identify problems of student performance.

2. The assessment assumes that the timely identification of problems permits timely and effective responses by the system. Therefore, the system must have a projection of where the students and teachers should be at any time of the year in each subject. The projections are important. If we don't know where the teacher should be at a particular time of year, we don't know where the kids should be. The more precise our expectations for kids of different ability levels, the more current we will be in being able to respond to problems. The response, of course, is to fix up the problem and keep the kids progressing on schedule.

3. The projections imply an instructional sequence that can be clearly calibrated into calendar time units. Ideally, the program would be divided into lessons or units that could be presented in class periods. After so many class periods or contact days, we would expect the kids to be at a certain lesson or unit, and we would expect them to pass the assessment measures that document their mastery of the material.

4. The system should accommodate kids of different ability levels and place them appropriately in material that matches their level of performance. Kids should be grouped homogeneously for instruction. Therefore, the system must have daily schedules that permit "cross-class" grouping in all major subjects. All classrooms in the primary grades, for instance, would teach arithmetic at the same time, so that kids from various classrooms could work in relatively homogeneous ability groups.

5. The assessment, projections, and schedules imply an instructional program that has the potential to teach all kids placed appropriately in the program. Such material is the keystone of the system. Without such materials, the other facets of the system become non-functional. There is little point in projecting where the kids should be after four months of instruction if the projection can be achieved by only a small percentage of the teachers and students. If the assessments of what students

have learned reveals only that students have many problems, the assessment instruments become relatively useless. Their purpose is to identify what we otherwise might not observe, and to imply a remedy. No clear remedy is implied if all the kids have problems (except to start over with something that works better).

- The program must have specific features that support quality-control. What is being taught must be clearly identifiable (or we can't test whether it's being taught).

- The program must also be "teachable," which means that the average teacher, with a reasonable amount of training, could present it so that the students uniformly meet projections. Uniformity is important. If the program design does not permit a very high percentage of teachers to meet projections, the quality-control system tends to collapse. Identifying problems with teachers becomes an empty ritual because training remedies are apparently not possible. Structural remedies (such as removing the teacher) are possible, but if these remedies are called for in a high percentage of cases, the program design is not appropriate for the system.

- If the program is teachable, we can assume that any problems the kids have imply a teacher-presentation problem. Student problems, therefore, are generally solved by fixing up how the teacher presents the material, not by redoing the material.

6. Given the five features of system listed above, it would be possible to play the game of quickly identifying "what's wrong with this picture." The features, however, imply someone who plays that game – the trainer, who works primarily in the classroom. By looking at the posted schedule on a classroom wall, the trainer can identify (a) how many days the students have been taught; and (b) what lesson or unit the students are currently working on. By comparing this information with the projection for the group, the trainer is able to identify whether students are as far as they are supposed to be. By observing

the teaching, the trainer is able to answer questions such as: Are the kids performing adequately on what they are currently being taught?

- If there are problems, the trainer can identify possible causes: Is the teacher following the specifications of the program? Are various teaching behaviors appropriate? The trainer can also determine problems by referring to the latest assessment of the kids' performance. That answers questions about precisely what the kids have trouble learning. Comparing test information with what the teacher does when teaching usually answers questions about the cause of the problem.

For the trainer to be effective, the trainer must have schedules and duties. Generally, the trainer would spend at least 70 percent of her time in contact with teachers, either in the classroom or in in-service sessions that focus on specific difficulties teachers are experiencing. The trainer would be expected to work individually with teachers on specific problems (demonstrating remedies with the kids if necessary, practicing with the teacher, providing follow ups and contacting the teacher to make sure that remedies are working).

The system described above is clean and workable within the framework of current performance levels of those who teach in schools. The system would provide ongoing advocacy for each student by assuring that projections are reasonable for that student, and by seeing to it that the projections are met. All the components of this system are referenced to the single purpose of responding intelligently to the problems that kids are experiencing and to assuring that all are being taught effectively. The system, therefore, is completely accountable because all of its assumptions are related to school practices. Neither kids nor their families are blamed for failure. Failures are assumed to be created by failures within the delivery system (given that the kids have been in school regularly).

Also, every component of the system is necessary. Removing or altering some components would not create a crash in the system, but it would create a need for increasingly elaborate and messy additions.

The quality-control system implies changes in governance and structure within the system.

1. The trainer must have authority to give teachers and principals assignments. The trainer cannot function as an advocate without this authority, because the powerless trainer will not be able to provide sensible, timely remedies to all problems that are identified. One type of problem is the resistant teacher who has not followed the program. If the kids are in trouble, the remedy begins with the clear statement that the teacher is to follow the program, or she will be reassigned. The trainer should have that authority. Another type of problem is the teacher who does not have the skills needed to present the material appropriately. The most efficient solution may be a "structural change," a modified schedule with the kids regrouped so they are taught effectively during the days that the trainer works with this teacher or seeks a replacement. The trainer should have the authority to change schedules, reassign students, or provide other modifications of the delivery system.

2. The accountability scheme within the system should parallel the allocations of authority. The role of the trainer implies "nested authority-accountability," in which teachers and principals have only one boss.

   - The teacher is responsible-accountable for the performance of all her students.

   - The principal is responsible-accountable for the performance of all her teachers and all her students.

   - The trainer (who may service between 3 and 5 schools) is responsible for all her principals, all her teachers, all her students.

   - The assistant superintendent is responsible for all her trainers, all her principals, all her teachers, all her students.

This simple pyramid of accountability keeps the system in focus and permits the quick identification of problems. In current systems, there are fragmented responsibilities. The principal in a larger system may work for 3 or 4 different assistant superintendents. The pyramid of accountability means both that problems will be addressed on the appropriate level of "authority" and that the practice for dealing with problems that are not immediately solved is to "bump it up." For example, a teacher in school **A** is having lots of problems. The assessment practices assure that the principal and the trainer are aware of the problem. The standard procedure is for the trainer to provide an assignment and the principal to monitor the classroom to verify whether the problem is being solved or tends to persist. If it persists, the principal reports to the trainer and the trainer is to respond with a more potent solution. If the problem is not solved in a timely manner, the trainer must bump the problem up to her boss. At this point, the trainer knows what the problem is and understands what the solution should be. The trainer has tried to exercise her authority, but the problem is one that goes beyond her authority. (Possibly it's a union related problem or a tenure problem that makes it impossible to remove or reassign a resistant teacher.)

What's bumped up to higher levels is always a problem that is not being solved on a lower level. This practice is reasonable because the only justification for higher levels in a quality-control system is to solve problems that are not solvable on the lower levels.

The nested responsibilities would also make it possible to streamline the central administration in larger districts – possibly eliminating more than half of the current personnel. There would not be multiple inputs to schools from the "chapter 1 coordinator," the "elementary supervisor," or some assistant superintendent in charge of "social studies" curriculum. For academic matters, the trainer is in charge. Extra-academic functions are scheduled in a way that they do not compromise the work on academics.

There would be great reduction in "special-ed" classes, remedial tracks, and classes that simply "reteach" material that was supposed to have been taught on earlier levels. So the plan represents both an economy in central personnel and an economy on the level of individual schools. If all schools in a district had this system in place, it would become far easier to place incoming students because a large percentage of them would come from a school that followed the same quality-control practices as the receiving school.

Rewards and punishment within the system are easily referenced to the responsibilities of the players.

1. Teachers who meet projections should be rewarded – individually – both with recognition and with monetary incentives. Teachers who exceed minimum expectations should receive additional incentives. Teachers who work with high-risk kids should receive a higher base than teachers who work with middle-class kids.

2. Principals and trainers should receive a base salary contingent on the percentage of students who meet or exceed expectations. The percentage would change according to the number of years the plan has been in place. During the first year, the percentage would be lower than it would during the second and third years. After the third year, the basis for retaining principals and trainers would be that about 90 percent of kids who had been in regular attendance met projections. Principals and trainers would receive bonuses for percentages over 94 percent. (These numbers would be adjusted downward for middle and secondary schools.)

3. Teachers, principals, and trainers should be reassigned or fired if they fail to achieve minimum performance standards with a specified percentage of students. The percentage of those reassigned would go up after the first year of implementation. A fair system would provide for some "probation" but not a lot because the system is referenced to kid performance, and if there isn't sufficient progress with the kids, those responsible for the delivery of instruction should be retrained or replaced. In an established system, failure to meet projections with at least 90 percent of the students would result in reassignment or dismissal.

Once the student-referenced system is in place, the system could dramatically influence other aspects of the educational system – publishers, colleges of education, professional groups, unions.

Training: Teachers must be trained; trainers must be trained. The colleges of education typically do not provide teachers who are well versed in the basic details of instruction. The school system should, therefore, serve as its own teacher-training institution and should not permit teachers to work in the system unless they pass performance standards for managing kids, presenting material appropriately, providing effective corrections, and reinforcing kids. This training would give local colleges of education immediate notice that their students are not sufficiently skilled.

Teacher training provided by the district would be referenced to the instructional programs the teachers were to use. The purpose of the training would be to assure that the teachers are proficient in the procedure formats that they would use in working with students. Ongoing in-service would address problems that students and teachers experience.

Trainers are most reasonably selected from teachers. The best teachers should be candidates for trainer positions. Before becoming a trainer, however, a good teacher must learn many skills that are not immediately obvious. A good training program would provide for superior teachers to spend an hour or two of the schoolday working with the trainer and possibly following up on assignments the trainer has issued. Again, the district could provide a strong message to the colleges of education by not hiring people with traditional administrative degrees.

Instructional approaches: Any instructional approach used in the elementary schools especially, would have to meet the requirements for the student-referenced system. It would have to be teachable by the average teacher, trainable by the average trainer, and manageable by the average supervisor. The system would not permit its installation until the instructional approach or program had been demonstrated to work well with students and teachers.

The system should have an ongoing "learner verification" effort for promising approaches (and variations of extant practices). Before an instructional program is installed, clearly stated benefits would be expressed. These could be provided by professional organizations, publishers, or teachers who believe that the approach has promise. The benefits of the approach would be clearly stated in terms of what the students would be taught within a specific time frame. The proposed approach could have the benefit of teaching a greater number of skills in less time; it could have the benefit of permitting acceleration with average performing students or with lower performers; it could have the benefit of requiring less teacher preparation, or of implying simplified monitoring.

Once the anticipated benefits have been articulated and related to the time line (when we will observe the benefit in teacher or student performance), the program is experimentally tried out with several teachers. The experiment is conducted with the clear understanding that if the program does not permit uniform training of teachers, it is not used with those who find it difficult to use; and if the program fails to achieve the promised benefits or achieves them at the price of important criteria achieved by the current approach, the experiment is immediately terminated. The program is rejected and the sponsoring group is provided with the performance information that is needed for them to consider possible revisions of the approach.

If the program comes close to meeting its promises, the program could then be expanded, with careful observations to determine teacher problems or possible downside effects with students.

If the program does well in the field-test, it could be adopted as either an option within the system or as the replacement approach.

This practice would provide publishers with clear information of what the system requires and what it does not accept. The "new copyright" on the program would not serve as an enticement for the system to try out the program; therefore, publishers who were interested in working with "world-class" schools would have to adopt "world-class" standards for developing and field-testing their programs.

The board, the administration, and the public: In an ideal system, the board would direct the administration in instructional matters, and not vice versa. The role of the board would be to state how student performance should change. The administration would provide honest and timely evaluations of the changes that are occurring. The public would receive honest and timely information about the status of students within the system and information about progress. In an ideal system, the public would become literate about educational practices because the system would be professional and would provide the public with valid information. There would be no redefinitions of reading, no suggestions that a process is installed because it is an end in itself, no adoption of half baked proposals, no hype for alternative schools that are strictly experimental.

Reports to the public and the board wouldn't be based solely on the assessments used for quality-control within the system, but would also use standardized assessments, such as those that are currently being developed for the Bush 2000 plan. Reports, however, would consider the results of the quality-control assessments as the primary indicators of student success because they show the extent to which students are learning the material presented in the instructional programs and sequences identified for use. The programs were selected because they held promise of teaching students a sequence of skills that was judged appropriate. Students who learn all the material in one of these programs, therefore, would be judged to have met a set of precise standards. The quality-control measures give information about this process.

The standardized measures don't provide insight into the teaching process but provide for comparisons of populations of students. They do not imply remedies as readily as the more precise measures because they provide only a sampling of this and that. They are subject to abuses because it would take a relatively short period of time to teach naive students the information they need to pass the test, compared to the amount of time required to prepare students for all the sub-tests of the quality-control assessment.

The standardized assessments are useful in showing trends of student performance and overall progress of different populations at different grades.

• • •

The sketch that I've provided treats the curriculum as the central focus of reform, because teachers don't teach without content. The content comes from the curriculum. The difference between the performance of a kid who performs "well" and one who does "poorly" can be expressed solely in terms of how much of the curriculum each kid mastered.

There can be no effective reform in the early grades (where the greatest failures occur) without recognizing the pre-eminent role of the curriculum and focusing the reform accordingly.

The problem with most current reform proposals (and the obvious reason they won't work) is that they do not recognize the role of the curriculum. Some educators promote systemic change, and they provide discussions of how assessment, school management, teacher motivation, school organization, and other issues are related to the process. But typically, their processes are fuzzy because their relationships between the teacher, the school, and instructional practices are unclear. An example is William Clune's *Systemic Educational Policy*. His position is reasonable. He supports the idea that there must be effective policy for improving instructional outcomes. He makes sensible observations, such as the idea that it's not reasonable to have a totally site-based management system. "…Instead of the unstructured free-for-all in local planning and discretion often associated with school-based management, we need exactly the opposite: a strong structure which allows teacher discretion to be exercised in the most productive manner."

He discusses the components of systemic policy, but the details of the system get away from him very quickly because he seems committed to the idea that teacher discretion and teacher autonomy are givens.

Clune apparently doesn't know the basic game of making kids smart, as he admits. "The most important reason for indicators of educational outcomes is our substantial and continuing ignorance about the determinants of student achievement." The determinants of student achievement are the details of the teaching.

Although Clune's systemic policies are fuzzy because they lack understanding of the central feature of instruction, Clune attempts to show how research and information on performance could be used to shape **policy** in school systems. This attempt is important. Currently there is no policy for managing instruction and student outcomes.

Chapter 14: Systematic Change

Other proposals are far more monolithic than Clune's. For instance, Jona than Kozol's *Savage Inequalities* reduces the question of reform to the question of discrimination, racial segregation, and fiscal inequities. Kozol questions whether the same assessments should be used for places like Mississippi, which are funded at less than $3,000 a year, and for kids from Great Neck, where kids are funded at $16,000 per year. Kozol also has the idea that Headstart will somehow make a difference. He asserts that Headstart is terrific and that every teacher knows that it is.

Kozol points out real inequities, but they are not the "causes" for the differences that Kozol observes. Headstart is not terrific and has not resulted in significant improvement of disadvantaged kids. The funding level in Mississippi might be a little light for creating an effective systemic-change model, but on its current budget, it could, within four years, pass up places like Detroit, Chicago, NYC, and LA, all of which have a substantially higher funding level. Money is important, but it is not the answer. Follow Through documented that. The kids in Follow Through were funded rather lavishly, compared to kids in regular-school programs. Yet, kids who were in models that focused on discovery and development performed more poorly than kids in traditional Title 1 programs.

Even Albert Shanker, president of the American Federation of Teachers, came out with an interesting proposal for reform. It's interesting because it places contingencies on performance. Unfortunately, it's based on serious misunderstanding of the problems. "The rigid and confining structure that the traditional model of education imposes on teachers and students doesn't enable even the majority of children to be educated – and it never did." True, but misleading. The implication that the "freed" teacher will solve problems of education is refuted by lots and lots of data.

Shanker's idea of education is opposed to the notion that views students as "vessels into which knowledge must be poured or as raw materials that the education process turns into finished products. But people become educated because of the work they do." The appeal is poetic, but it serves as an excuse for failing to teach. What follows from Shanker's conception of the teacher's role is that current failures are caused by the students. They didn't become educated. Therefore, they must have failed to do what they needed to do.

Despite this sorting-machine logic, Shanker's proposal calls for schools that are classified as "winners and losers." His plan is basically to give all schools a free reign, reward winners and punish the losers. The winners could be the highest ten percent of participating schools in the U.S., after a five-year period. "The winners would receive cash awards, distributed to all school members." The losers? "...the most miserable schools ought to be closed...teachers from a failed school would be back on the hiring line."

Come on, Al. Although this proposal is bold and indicates that the American Federation of Teachers is willing to negotiate on teacher-performance standards and contingencies, the plan is best described by the word, "phew." Let's wait five years to find out what is happening. Let's then pay off ten percent of the schools – even the teachers in these schools that didn't contribute to the improvement. Let's put teachers back on the hiring line, even though individual teachers in the line may have had nothing to do with the decisions.

Shanker has the dream of the school in which "Team members will read, talk together, conduct school-level research and evaluations, and try out new ideas." And a Star will Rise in the East. What's the probability of a committee working? How long after school are teachers going to stay to work on this plan, so that five years from now, they'll get the big ten percent?

The proposal by President Bush for America 2000 is based on the idea that reform hinges on assessment. The national assessment of performance is supposed to make everybody aware of the problems, and provide a nation-wide comparison of performance of educational efforts. This national performance information will ostensibly shock our consciousness and spark new, innovative reforms. Sure thing. Measurement and assessment are needed components. They will show that the teaching is not effective. If the teaching is not effective, the most direct implication is that the curricular sequences are not well designed. Until we reach the curricula, we will not have discovered the problem. The problem is not global; it's technical. It's not some tabloid-like motivation or doing more homework, or reading to children. It's specific, like the details of how something is presented and reviewed. The Bush proposal will provide better knowledge of what kids are doing, but it will not teach teachers or administrators very much about how to correct the problem. After all, we've been deluged with data about our kids' academic failure for years. Since 1981, scarcely a week goes by without another comparison that shows U.S. kids slipping. Has this incessant data sparked "innovation"? It has sparked organizations like the NCTM, the NCTE, and the International Reading Association to adopt untried practices that retreat from the problems and create inevitable teacher and kid failure. It has sparked voluminous rhetoric, debate, and plans based on fantastic conceptions of what teachers and kids really are. And it has sparked much discrimination in the form of placing unprotected kids in classrooms that present material that mystifies them and confuses them about what they are to learn or even what they are supposed to do in school. Even the NAEP evaluations did little more than prompt irresponsible decisions, like Honig's installation of his junior-high math program, which had never been demonstrated to work well.

Effective reform must start with the understanding that the curriculum is the central focus and the central business of the schools. Effective curricula are the sine qua non of the system that is capable of delivering a quality education to all kids. For the delivery system to work, there must be policy that prevents academic child abuse and that closely links the motivation and interest of teachers and administrators with the academic success of kids.

CHAPTER 15

HOW CAN WE GET THERE FROM HERE?

Chapter 14 describes features and functions of a system that is referenced to students, but Chapter 14 doesn't indicate how the systemic change would occur (or if it can occur). As the earlier chapters suggest, the journey from where we are to a more sensitive system is arduous at best. Ironically, however, it's a journey that could be completed quickly (possibly in three or four years) once all the maps and ground rules are worked out.

In some cases, the school district may be cooperative in working out the ground rules, but more likely, the plan will represent a serious threat to the administration because it will call for many administrators and administrative functions to be scrapped. It's hard to imagine how a group of superintendents is going to say, "Oh, please reform our school system so that you can fire us." In many districts, however, that is what must happen.

The starting point is six basic restrictions that the school district must honor if significant reform is to follow:

1. Don't install any practice or reform unless you have substantial reason to believe that it will result in improvement of student performance;
2. Don't install any approach without making projections about student learning;
3. Don't install any practice without monitoring it and comparing performance in the classroom with projections;
4. Don't install an approach without having a back-up plan;
5. Don't maintain practices that are obviously not working as planned;
6. Don't blame parents, kids, or other extraneous factors if the plan fails.

Chapter 15: How Can We Get There From Here?

If the district honored these **don'ts**, the administration would be on the same side as the kids.

To guarantee alignment of the administration's interests with those of kids, administrators must suffer when the kids fail.

The details of this contingency would vary according to the contractual agreements that the district has with various superintendents and other central administrators, but the basic form would be: all administrators associated with a failed reform are fired or removed from their decision making positions. (They demonstrated, after all, that they are not expert at making predictions or at selecting approaches that have promise. They should be replaced with administrators who are more competent.)

The Business Roundtable and similar groups emphasize that winners should be rewarded and losers punished. Shanker's proposal punishes the entire staff for failure. The plan that I've outlined follows the same reward-punishment theme, but it places the principle contingency where it should be, **with those who are primarily responsible for educational practices and programs in the district**. The teachers are victims. They do either what they've been permitted to do or what they've been told to do. Their inability to teach well is no more their fault than the failure of minority kids is their fault. The segment of the school system that is at fault is clearly the decision makers. The public has responded to their proposals and plans as if they are thoughtful, knowledgeable suggestions, based on reasonable practices for protecting children and their parents. Wrong on all counts. The teachers take heat for doing a poor job when an initiative fails, but a major cause of their failure is the programs and procedures that were installed from above.

Nested accountability starts at the top, with the district superintendent. If the superintendent's job is on the line, the district will tend to be much more scrupulous about finding out what works. If underling superintendents associated with the reform were to be sent out to pasture or reassigned to the classroom following failure of a reform, they too would do whatever they could to see to it that their reform was a success. They would tend to "look before they leap," and be much more suspicious of "standards" and practices presented by groups like the NCTM and other teacher groups.

Possibly the most attractive feature of the accountability system for superintendents and administrators is that neither the board nor the public needs to be concerned with the administration's rhetoric. Historically, this rhetoric has intimidated parents and the public. When a respected "educator" indicates that a plan is based on new research about the development of the brain, the typical parent is not in a good position to say, "Baloney," but odds are pretty good that it is baloney. With the bet-your-job-on-your-reform format, nobody has to attend to the rhetoric. Say what you will about your theory; then follow the six don'ts and prove your point.

That's similar to the practice that we would follow in hiring a coach. If the coach had some apparently strange ideas about training or executing on the playing field, we wouldn't have to make a decision about their validity on the basis of rhetoric. There is a playing field that is capable of providing pretty clear evidence. Let the games begin.

1. **Don't install an approach unless you have substantial reason to believe that it will result in improved student performance.**

A good plan is to require the administration to show that the plan works on a small scale before using it across the board. The small-scale tryout would give the administration a chance to test out different approaches. Even though failure in a small-scale tryout is more humane than failure in an entire school district, children should not be guinea pigs for mindless experiments that have little hope of working. The small-scale tryout is not to be a learning experience for the administration as it discovers facts that it should already know. Therefore, the board should limit the number of tryout programs that are permitted, and should establish contingencies for failure. In a larger district, like San Francisco, the board might permit experimenting with 2 or 3 approaches for reading in the primary grades. The board, however, should require the administration to contact successful teachers within the district and solicit their advice and guidance before installing any approach. (These are teachers who consistently produce results that are above the demographically predicted level.)

Chapter 15: How Can We Get There From Here?

Each tryout should involve possibly three classrooms on the same grade levels. The reason for different classrooms is to identify possible problems of "uniformity," and to get a better idea of what type of teacher training is required for successful implementation.

It's possible that the administration feels it has sufficient data to embark on a large-scale implementation. The decision should not be left entirely to the administration. If the board agrees that the data is compelling, however, the district could begin an implementation that involves a substantial number of schools.

2. Don't install an approach without making projections about student learning.

Unless the benefits of the approach can be readily measured in terms of student outcomes, and unless they are outcomes we are concerned with, the administration should not be permitted to install the approach. Tests are needed to tell whether the students (and the administrators) succeed, or whether they fail.

The most obvious strategy would be to move cautiously; however, a possible problem is that administrators would become so cautious that nothing happens. Therefore, they must be told that they will engage in some installations, either small-scale or larger scale, within a particular time frame. The directive from the board may even indicate which areas must be addressed immediately. The prime candidates are:

>Initial reading (grades K through 3);
>
>Spelling (grades 3 through 8);
>
>Math (grades K through 3);
>
>Math (grades 4 through 6);
>
>Writing (grades 3 through 6);
>
>Corrective spelling, math, reading (grades 6 through 12).

The district could address all of these problems simultaneously. Note that none of them involves a full "series." Publishers market series that typically span grade levels 1-6 or 1-8. The district typically buys the series and installs it in all grade levels. This practice makes very little sense, because if the program is better than the programs currently in use, the students in the higher grades couldn't possibly match up with the grade-level designations of the program. Typical fifth graders in math perform on what would amount to the third or fourth level of a reasonably constructed instructional program. These kids would have great difficulty in the fifth level of a well-designed series. Therefore, why buy the fifth level now? Why try to install it now when the third or fourth level will accommodate the present fifth graders?

The targets that I've indicated for initial reform are important and manageable. Cleaning up seventh-grade math would be a headache because of the discrepancy between the skills assumed by the instructional material and the skills of the kids. This is not to say that we should forget about the seventh grade. It's simply easier to start where the problems start – in the earliest grades. The information we receive about the approach we install will be a lot cleaner.

Before the approach is installed, the administration **must make projections**. Projections should be made for students of high-ability, middle ability, and low-ability. For middle-ability and low-ability students, one of the goals may simply be a significant reduction in the number of students who fail. For instance, at the end of the first-grade year, there should be no children who cannot decode. The test is **oral reading** of a passage such as the one below:

> That man has a big kite. We went up the hill with him. Then he showed us how to make a kite go up and up. His string did not hold the kite. And the kite went down, down. We ran after it When we went home, we made a big, big kite.

Kids who make more than 4 or 5 decoding errors fail. The administration should predict the maximum number (or percentage) of reading failures that will be observed at the end of the first-grade year. (The percentage of students passing should not be below 92%.) A similar test (with harder words) could be presented at the end of the second-grade year. (The words used in the tests should be words taught in the instructional program.)

The board should not accept projections that are based solely on any instrument that can easily be "taught to," such as an achievement test. The primary test should be a "do it" test – that requires actual reading, answering questions, working math problems, and so forth — not multiple choice items. There should be simple, alternative forms of whatever is used to test the students so that we can determine that the kids' test performance is a valid indicator of what had been taught. (If we have doubts, we present one or more of the alternative forms.)

The projections for the new program should be related to current performance. Therefore, reasonable instruments should be developed or adopted, and a reasonable sample of students should be thoroughly evaluated. Expect this evaluation to reveal student problems that are not evident from standardized-test performance. Also, expect the students' performance to be even worse than anticipated.

While the details of the projections may get sticky, the board should not accept the administration's projections for modest improvement. We can get modest improvement by testing the kids from time to time, or by improving the incentive system (giving them a dollar for every unit they complete, or something similar). The reform must take a large step toward world-class standards.

3. Don't install any practice without monitoring it and comparing performance in the classroom with projections.

The monitoring is necessary for the administration that wants the program to succeed. The administration should be quite willing to work with the teachers involved in the implementation and provide whatever knowledge and skills are needed for them to zip through the adopted curricular sequence. If the administration is foolish, it will implement initially with its best teachers. This mistake will result in the administration receiving a seriously distorted view of what level of training and monitoring is needed for the program to work uniformly.

Part of the monitoring should document the extent to which teachers follow designated procedures and schedules. The schedule aspect is very important. During the '70s it was fashionable for districts to make up their own science or social studies programs. Some science programs required the teacher to spend about two hours a day on science. That's against the rules of the current reform game. The installed programs must be limited to a reasonable period of time. For reading, no kid in grades 1-3 should spend more than an hour a day on reading instruction.

The monitoring should also deal with what the teachers do and how it relates to what the kids have learned. Weekly evaluations indicate whether the projected material is presented on schedule, whether the teachers need significant help, and whether they are faithfully following the program.

There are many possible outcomes and implications. For the ideal situation, the teachers didn't need a lot of additional training; the training they needed is manageable; there seemed to be uniform success among the teachers; the daily schedules provided sufficient time for the material to be presented; and the kids (even the lower performers) mastered the material in the projected time frame.

The program could "bomb" along any of these dimensions. If the teachers couldn't be uniformly trained or the training required unreasonable amounts of time, the program would have a seriously qualified potential. If the program didn't work well for the full range of students, it failed with the lower performers. If it's not appropriate for them, we are no closer to finding a solution for them. (And they may constitute the largest problem and the largest population of students we work with.)

Teachers who received training may not have found it possible to teach the units in the allotted time. Although the students may have learned the material that had been presented, the rate of presentation may have been slow enough to cause students to fall far behind projections. A tough decision would be whether the program is still worth the benefits it provides.

Lots of other contingencies are possible; lots of other implications result. However, in most cases, it should be fairly apparent whether or not the program achieved results that are superior to those of current practices.

4 & 5. Don't install an approach without having a back-up plan, and don't maintain failed plans.

Part of the initial plan should have a "pull-the-plug" criterion and a backup plan. The criterion should be expressed in a way that permits some flexibility, but that requires an empathic response to kid problems. For example, after four months, the lower performers must have uniformly learned a certain set of skills. The administration must anticipate that this outcome may not be achieved and therefore an **intelligent** back-up plan would be used. Similarly, after the teachers in the tryout have received a total of so many "training" hours, the plug is pulled on the training (because it is going beyond reasonable limits). If students don't perform according to projections following the termination of teacher training, the plug is pulled on the approach. Again, a plan B must be available.

The pull-the-plug criteria should be set for different time periods, because it's possible for the instructional approach to start out acceptably and then falter seriously. What we don't want the administrators to do is to leave students in the approach all year long and then at the end of the year conclude that it was a bomb.

6. **Don't blame parents, kids, or other extraneous factors if the plan fails.**

The plan is undertaken with an understanding of how the kids currently perform, about the demography of the parents, and other factors. These factors should be clearly assumed by the plan. The only factor that affects the plan is whether the kids and the teacher are in attendance on a regular basis. Aside from unusual situations, this is the only consideration that should be used to demur the results of the implementation. If the teaching failed, it was because the teaching failed, not because the parents didn't get involved.

• • •

This plan for identifying and installing superior curricula involves orchestrating details. An argument against the process is that the details are time consuming. Actually, all the details named in this plan are those that would be expected to be in place in any system that was concerned with teaching kids effectively and eliminating academic child abuse.

A large part of today's educational problems results from the absence of these details. Today's reforms are often studies in global good will. Bush's 2000 plan is an example. Everybody gets together with a lot of good will and thinks positively about literacy and success, and everything turns out rosy.

A solid quality-control system would provide a definitive basis for evaluating proposals related to "teacher autonomy" or site-based decision making. Teachers could be permitted to work in teams and use whatever approach is appropriate for doing their own thing. So long as projections were clearly related to a time line, the district could run a test that would provide all the information any administrator would ever need about why the plan will not work and why autonomous units are not only highly inefficient but create such variability from teacher to teacher that student failure is guaranteed in a fairly high percentage of classrooms.

The quality-control system could be used by local and state boards of education for dealing with outside contractors. While the issues of governance vary from state to state, it's generally possible for local boards of education to contract with parties other than the school district. The contract should indicate the benefits in terms of student performance and should provide a time table. The installation of the plan should be carefully monitored, and it should not be continued when the monitoring discloses that it is not working as promised.

On the level of the state and professional organizations, similar quality control practices should be followed. The NCTM, for instance, should be required to test out its elementary-school "standards" following the provisions outlined for the school-district plan. In absence of such data, the organization should be labelled as what it is: a promoter of opinion and possible academic child abuse. There are no pure-food laws to protect teachers and students against the incredible nostrums that these organizations generate. Advocacy groups like The International Institute for Advocacy for School Children disseminate some information, but there are no formal contingencies that require professional groups to behave in a professional manner. If we are to purge these organizations of irresponsible practices, we must install policy that takes the place of "laws," and we must actively support such policy.

CHAPTER 16
YOU

No laws exist to combat academic child abuse. Educational decision makers and professional groups are able to promote practices that are ineffective and that lead to failure. Decision makers routinely select these practices over those that require a realistic solution, primarily because the realistic solution requires what the decision makers and the system do not have: technical understanding and the structure needed to implement quality-control measures.

Do not underestimate the insidious qualities of the system. I know dozens of war stories about effective teachers — ones who achieve super results — being removed from committees, being censured for stating obvious facts of failures to supervisors, and even being fired for telling the truth. The system is not greatly tolerant of individual dissenters. In California, for instance, there are thousands of teachers who are perfectly aware of the failure of whole-language in the primary grades — teachers who grumble, complain, and confide about their instructional problems with other teachers. The number of teachers who would protest on behalf of the children, however, is roughly the same as the number of principals who protested the illegal practices of the state. The system is strong, and although it appears to be open to negotiations, it is extremely rigid. In places like Houston, where Direct-Instruction practices have recently received publicity for producing superior results, the middle management of the school system is very active in restoring the party line and lobbying to discredit the hard work of people who should be held up as exemplars of effective teaching practices with at-risk kids.

The system will not change without serious pressure from outside. The pressure must be both clearly and narrowly focused. That focus should be on establishing minimum quality-control measures and accountability procedures that protect children and their families from unnecessary failure. The focus is implied by the basic **don'ts** about installing practices without first showing that they are effective and having a sensible backup plan.

Chapter 16: You

Here are some specific things that you can do either as a concerned citizen or as member of a group.

1. **Read.** While a large segment of the public is both literate and concerned, the public does not read the drivel that the system writes. I honestly don't know how any literate adult could read the material published by California and not see incredible contradictions and gaping holes that are filled with raging rhetoric and magic.

Don't rely on summaries provided by the press. The educational press may be a reliable source of information about problems and the poor performance of students. On matters of reform, however, the educational press is not very literate. Investigative reporting on issues associated with reform is something that simply doesn't exist.

If you want to find out what's happening, you should read the documents put out by your educational systems. In most cases, you'll find incredible slippage. The most common pattern starts with a state legislature that requires reform. The mandate goes to the State Board, which kicks it over to the Department of Education, which reduces it, dilutes it, displaces, and perverts it until it is a reform of the dimensions the system can accommodate.

In Ohio, for example, the legislature mandated phonics instruction in grades one through three for at least 15 minutes a day. Part of the legislation ordered the State Board to adopt whatever regulations were necessary to implement this law. The Board was also charged with specifying programs and providing training. Naturally, the Board turned the task over to the state Department of Education. The result was a rather thorough redefinition of phonics and guidelines that dealt with none of the issues that one would imagine for "guidelines." Here is a draft of the guidelines for implementing phonics:

Rules for Phonics.

A. The Ohio State Board of Education shall formulate and prescribe minimum standards requiring the use of phonics as a technique in the teaching of reading in grades Kindergarten through three.

B. As used in this rule, the term "phonics" means the relationship between letters, speech sounds, patterns, and meaning units such as prefixes, suffixes, and root words in written language.

C. Phonics instruction shall be based on the child's understanding of essential concepts (such as print directionality, what a word is, letter knowledge, and that print carries the message).

D. Phonics instruction shall occur in meaningful contexts and may consist of a combination of several of the following activities:

   1. **Illustrating** the relationships between letters of the alphabet and sounds utilizing words in the spoken language of the student; how vowels and consonants blend to form syllables; and how syllables form words.

   2. Reading aloud to children to heighten awareness of the link between written and spoken language.

   3. Providing frequent opportunities for students to read and to re-read books and materials to practice and apply their understanding of phonics.

   4. Developing the ability of students to approximate word pronunciation by applying phonic generalizations.

   5. Demonstrating letter-sound relationships using familiar words as concrete examples.

   6. Showing students how to compare unknown words with similarly spelled familiar words to help recognize unknown words.

   7. Utilizing knowledge of letter-sound relationships, **meaning of text**, and structure of words to help students to recognize unknown words.

E. Phonics instruction functions as a technique to help students construct meaning from text and to develop independence in learning.

F. The state Board of Education shall provide in-service training programs for teachers on the use of phonics as a technique in the teaching of reading in grades Kindergarten through three.

Step B defines phonics in a way that is perfectly preposterous. Phonics is not "the relationship between letters, speech sounds, patterns, and meaning units such as prefixes, suffixes,..." Phonics deals only with words that are phonically regular. Most "affixes" are anything but regular. (The ending of words like **mission** and **vacation** are not phonically regular.)

The recommended activities in Step D are not serious phonics practices.

Activity 1 involves illustrating relationships between letters, sounds, syllables, etc. Syllables can either be phonically regular or not.

Activity 2 is reading aloud to children to heighten awareness between written and spoken language. Get the hook. This has absolutely nothing to do with phonics.

Activity 3 (providing opportunities for students to read and re-read) has very little to do with teaching phonics. This activity assumes phonics has already been taught.

Activity 4 is an activity of a different color. "Developing the ability of students to approximate word pronunciation by applying phonic generalizations." What kind of activity is that? It is actually not an activity, but rather the goal of phonics instruction.

Activity 6 (showing students how to compare unknown words with similarly spelled familiar words) could have very little to do with phonics unless the words are phonetically regular. The words **to**, and **do** are spelled similarly. Comparing them with **no** would have little **to do** with phonics.

A lot of problems could have been avoided if the literate public had responded to what the department proposed. Certainly, not everybody would be interested in reading this stuff, but if even one percent of the public read and respond, many problems could be aborted.

2. **Write and call.** Schools and school administrations are political. If you make a loud enough noise, the schools will respond. Districts could not get away with much of what they do if an informed public called them on their more obvious lapses into fantasy. The simplest way to protest what seems

to be a "redefinition" by the administration is to call or write the administration and the board. In Ohio, for example, a caller might question who hired the people in the Department of Education who made up the implementation guidelines. A letter to the board could state that the department is not performing and should be required to specify activities that meet the approval of teachers who know what phonics is.

3. **Confront decision makers.** There are meetings in which boards and administrations formalize, report, and adopt proposals and policies. These are often open to the public. However, the public either doesn't show up, or shows up to discuss some agenda item other than the ones involving instruction and management. I don't think the public was represented at the hearing in California where whole-language textbooks were adopted. Yet, the meeting was open to the public. If several groups of people had shown up and presented petitions demanding the board to adopt programs that work and to "withhold" immersion into literature until it could demonstrate that it worked, the board would have listened. Boards respond to numbers.

4. **If performance of students is poor, petition boards to provide alternatives other than contracts with the school district.** In most cases, the school board has the arbitrament needed to contract with outside agencies. There are groups that would provide clear, guaranteed-performance instruction for kids who are in regular attendance (such as the Association for Direct Instruction). If the Department of Education was in strict competition with such an organization, rhetoric would tend to give way to more relevant facts and figures. If the contracting organization worked in grades K through 3, it could provide the board and the district with a "second opinion" – both about what can be achieved with students and what sorts of controls and procedures are needed for such success.

5. **Petition boards to require school districts to provide accurate and detailed assessments of how kids perform on basic skills.** Petition boards to require the district to use this information and refer to it in formulating plans and making

predictions about success. This step is extremely important. So long as the district has no basis for assessing performance of students, it has no memory. Therefore, it has no methods for mapping its progress in solving problems. The district must have a memory of what it did and how the practice worked. The district must not revert back to failed practices even when they reappear with new labels.

6. **Petition boards to focus on the primary grades.** The district should not be permitted to install **any** program across the board without documenting that it works. The district's most common rejoinder will be that the cost of actually testing materials with teachers and kids is excessive. The cost is actually much less than the cost of an instructional sequence that doesn't work and that will not be replaced for five years or more.

A good plan would be not to believe whatever learner-verification data the publisher provided (even for programs that have substantial learner-verification data), and to test all programs. Recommendations by "teacher committees" for adopting untested programs should be vigorously protested as mindless experimentation unless those on the committee have provided clear demonstrations that they are superior teachers. (Teachers who have not taught effectively in the past should not be permitted to rely on their opinions for the simple reason that their opinions have been demonstrated to be unreliable indicators of what works.)

7. **Align with advocacy groups.** There are various groups that purport to be advocates for school children. Most, however, do not focus on basic practices that schools must follow to avoid academic child abuse. The International Institute for Advocacy for School Children does. Its message is simply that whatever works well is fine and schools should use it; however, they must demonstrate that the practices achieve world-class goals and that they are working adequately with all teachers and kids. If inferior practices are being maintained, the district is guilty of academic child abuse and has a serious moral obligation to terminate those practices.

I'ASC is also concerned with academic discrimination, which most seriously affects children who are at risk. The Urban League and NAACP have a history of working on problems of visible discrimination (such as hiring practices); however, they have not addressed discriminatory practices used by educational systems, such as shoving more homework on kids (with the idea that the parents are responsible for doing the teaching) or blaming parents for the fact that the schools are not doing well with minority kids.

If parents in your area are concerned with performance of kids in the schools (a mysteriously high rate of "dyslexia," for instance), you may want to form a local chapter of I'ASC.

Contact I'ASC for details:

>   International Institute for Advocacy for School Children
>
>   296 w. 8th
>
>   Eugene, OR 97401
>
>   Phone:503-485-6349 Fax: 503-683-7543

I'ASC has several consultants. One of them may be able to come to your district, conduct some observations, and provide the board with a second opinion on what is happening in the schools and the extent to which it is creating or maintaining academic child abuse.

One advantage in working with an organization like I'ASC is that the district is often proficient at putting others on the defensive and using rhetoric to support its conclusions. I'ASC can cut through the rhetoric and express the problem in terms of whether there is a problem and what sort of basic procedures are needed for the district to discover the solution. (If the procedures are not in place, the discovery will not occur.)

If you're the parent of a primary-grade kid, you may have a far more tightly-focused interest in the schools. Here are some suggestions for protecting your kid:

1. **Try to get the facts.** Find out what kind of instruction the school is using for reading, math, and science. What are the schedules? What is the performance of the class? How does

that performance relate to other classes? How does that performance relate to the "national norms"? The principal may not be able to answer these questions, but if enough people are asking them and are not very pleased with the responses, the principal may get the idea that he should have the answers. He's running the school, and it's very difficult to run an operation without having specific information about how the operation is performing.

2. **Observe.** Make arrangements to see what's happening in the classroom. Spend a morning and take notes. See how much time is spent on reading, how frequently each kid is "called on" or responds, how much time is spent on activities that do not seem to be related to identifiable skills.

3. **Reject sorting-machine excuses for failure.** If your kid is not reading by the end of the first grade and if the kid is not retarded (IQ below 75), do not accept excuses that blame the kid.

    a. **The kid has dyslexia.** One of the greatest myths perpetrated by the establishment is dyslexia. You've probably seen fanciful television commercials that show jumbled, upside-down and backwards symbols and declare that this is how reading looks to some children. Wrong. The symbols look no different to those children than they do to any other kids. There is precisely nothing wrong with the "dyslexic" kid except that the teaching failed. Understand that there are institutions and societies (such as the Orton Society) that are devoted to "dyslexia." Also understand that dyslexia is real in the sense that kids who do not learn to read are obviously confused about what reading is. But the assumption of the label dyslexia is that the kid is at fault — not that the kid has been the victim of academic child abuse. We have worked with thousands of kids and have never seen one who failed to learn to read when the teaching and management details are in place. We've worked with several hundred kids whose IQ was below 80 and every one was able to learn to read by the end of the first grade.

b. The kid has a **"specific learning disability," "a perceptual handicap, "suffers from "neurological immaturity, " "lack of readiness," or "emotional problems."**

These are after-the-fact labels that have been selected after the kid has failed. Perceptual handicapping conditions are largely a myth. If the kid can find his or her desk without groping around the room for a while, the kid can be taught to read. The label of "specific learning disability" is probably the greatest contradiction in the traditional educator's repertoire of labels. A kid can have a specific learning disability only if there is an unanticipated discrepancy between the kids' overall "readiness" performance, his performance in other subjects, and his performance in reading. In other words, the kid was perfectly "ready" for reading according to the school's readiness measures, but has failed to read.

The school predicted that the kid would learn, but is now faced with a kid who didn't learn. To solve that problem, the school invokes the label "specific learning disability," rather than label the kid as a casualty of poor instruction.

There are labels for math that parallel those for reading. The kid who can't perform in math is labelled "dyscalculic," which means that the kid can't calculate. Like the other labels, they are baloney. (Oscar Shaaf testified that he believed in dyscalculia, for whatever that's worth.)

c. **Scenarios about mysterious "growth rates" of kids.** A lot of whole-language implementations produce large numbers of non-readers by the end of the first grade. Often, teachers tell parents not to worry because these kids will catch up by the fourth grade. That's a flat-out lie. The truth is that the reading performance of kids by the middle of the first grade is highly predictive of their fourth-grade performance (particularly the kids who are not reading). The human side of this prediction is that the kids are confused, and unless successful communication with the kid is established, the kid will continue to be confused.

4. **In interactions with the board and administration, make it clear that the burden of proof for the programs and instructional practices in the schools rests with them.** Try to find out the basis they have for adopting the programs they use. Be careful about getting into a "research" discussion with the system. Keep the discussion very concrete, focusing on issues like: What firsthand evidence do you have to make you think that this approach is working? What is the failure rate now, compared to what it had been? You will probably become frustrated with the responses because the administration will run through the complete list of excuses, from lack of funds to the changing demography. In the end, stick to the central theme that the district should not be permitted to install and maintain practices that have not been shown to be superior.

5. **For upcoming adoptions of instructional materials, find out if the textbooks recommended for adoption were field-tested by the publisher before publication.** If **yes**, what were the results, and what learner-verification data is there to suggest that the program is superior to current practices? If **no**, what data does the selection committee have to support their belief in the program? How predictive is their judgment about what works based on examination of material? If they don't know how predictive it is, why are they using possibly unreliable methods for selecting instructional materials?

6. **Lobby to establish a district rule that no programs will be considered for adoption unless the district or another reliable agency has demonstrated that they work well.** The administration will vigorously protest such regulations, but that's tough. The still-wet copyright on an instructional program does not suggest that it is an improvement over anything.

7. **If your kid is a non-reader and you are not satisfied that the school is capable of correcting the problem, teach the kid your self. It's really not that hard.** The best program I know of is *Teach Your Child to Read in 100 Easy Lessons*, published by Simon & Schuster. I'm co-author of this program, but my purpose in recommending it is not to promote sales.

The program works. It's an adaptation of *DISTAR Reading*. It will teach the kid more about reading in 100 lessons than traditional basals teach in two school years. You can use the program with five year olds or even younger kids. If you follow the program specifications, the kid will read pretty well after 100 days of instruction. Some parents who are in districts that use whole-language teach their kids to read before they enter the first grade. These kids do just fine in whole-language.

• • •

At present, there are strong advocacy groups for the spotted owl, the killer whale, the Alaska fur seal, and hundreds of other "endangered species." Paradoxically, millions of our kids are endangered. They will fail in school. They will suffer a very real form of child abuse. Yet these kids have far less real advocacy than the spotted owl does. Rhetoric abounds, but the fact is that decisions affecting their academic future are made by dilettantes whose behavior strongly suggests that they are far more concerned with their own status than they are with saving kids. Furthermore, their stance is perfectly contradictory. They suggest that all kids can learn: however. their reforms provide demonstrations of student failure, not success. Their failures represent a serious form of abuse.

This situation doesn't have to be. Our kids can succeed, even those born in poverty. Our kids can receive the support, sensible legislation, and the kind of monitoring that other endangered species receive. But such advocacy will not come about from the establishment. It won't happen unless you help make it happen.

REFERENCES

Perspective

Abt Associates. 1977. *Education as experimentation: A planned variation model* (Vol. IV). Cambridge, MA: Abt Associates.

Anti Defamation League of B'nai B'rith. (1966). T*echniques for teaching arithmetic* [Film]. New York: Author.

House, E., Glass, G., McLean, L. & Walker, D. (1978). No simple answer: Critique of the 'Follow Through' evaluation. *Harvard Educational Review, 48*, 128-160.

USDE-OSEP. (1985-present). Instruction leadership training in special education. Eugene, OR: University of Oregon.

Chapter 2

Watson, D., Goodman, K., Freeman, Y., Murphy, S., & Shannon, P. (1987). *Report card on basal readers: The report of the commission on reading*. Washington DC: National Council of Teachers of English.

Chapter 3

Altwerger, B., Edelsy, C., & Flores, B. (1987). Whole language: What's new? *Reading Teacher*, 41(2), 144-154.

Commission on Reading, (1984). *Becoming a nation of readers: The report of the commission on reading*. Washington DC: US Department of Education.

Engelmann, S., & Bruner, E. C. (1988). *Reading mastery: Fast Cycle (DISTAR)*. Chicago, IL: Science Research Associates.

Goodman, K., & Goodman, Y. (1981). Twenty questions about teaching language. *Educational Leadership*, 38(6), 437-442.

Guthrie, J. (1981). Reading in New Zealand: achievement and volume. *Reading Research Quarterly*, 17(1), 6-27.

Langacker, R. (1973). *Language and its structure: Some fundamental linguistic concepts.* (2nd ed.). New York: Harcourt, Brace, Jovanovich.

Science Research Associates. (1989). *Corrective reading*. Chicago, IL: Author.

Chapter 4

Buckley, M. (Opening speaker). (July 20, 1988). *English-language arts SMC public input session* [Cassette]. Sacramento, CA: California State Department of Education.

Kim, Y., Berger, B., & Kratochvil, D. (1972). Distar instructional system—developed by Siegfried Engelmann & associates. In *It works*. Palo Alto, CA: American Institute for Research in the Behavioral Sciences.

California State Department of Education. (1988). *Building a quality English-language arts program*. Sacramento CA: Author.

References

Commission on Reading, (1984). *Becoming a nation of readers: The report of the commission on reading.* Washington DC: US Department of Education.

Engelmann, S., & Bruner, E. C. (1988). *Reading mastery: Fast Cycle (DISTAR).* Chicago, IL: Science Research Associates.

English-Language Arts Curriculum Framework and Criteria Committee. (1987). English-language arts framework for California public schools kindergarten through grade twelve. Sacramento CA: California State Department of Education.

Office of Curriculum Framework and Textbook Development. (1987). California instructional materials law. Sacramento CA: California State Department of Education.

Chapter 5

Barr, M. (1988, March). *Implementing a research-based curriculum in English-language arts, K-12.* Paper presented at the state staff development and curriculum conference, Pacific Grove, CA.

Beck, I., Perfetti, C., & McKeown, M. (1982). Effects of long-term vocabulary instruction on lexical access and reading comprehension. *Journal of Educational Psychology, 74,* 506-521.

Bussis, A., Chittenden, E., Amarel, M., & Klausner, E. (1985). *Inquiry into meaning: An investigation of learning to read.* Hillsdale NJ: Lawrence Erlbaum Associates.

California State Department of Education. (1988). *Building a quality English-language arts program.* Sacramento CA: Author.

Commission on Reading, (1984). *Becoming a nation of readers: The report of the commission on reading.* Washington DC: US Department of Education.

Engelmann, S. (June 10, 1988). Letter to F. Tempes, Assistant Superintendent of Instruction, State of California.

Engelmann, S. (July 14, 1988). Letter to F. Tempes, Assistant Superintendent of Instruction, State of California.

Galeano, K. (1983). Mother goose in the ESL classroom. In California State Department of Education. (1988). *Building a quality English-language arts program.* Sacramento CA: Author.

Gonzales, P. (1988, March). *Equity and access in a language arts program for all students.* Paper presented at the state staff development and curriculum conference, Pacific Grove, CA.

Langer, J. Envisionment: A reader-based view of comprehension. In California State Department of Education. (1988). *Building a quality English-language arts program.* Sacramento CA: Author.

Office of Curriculum Framework and Textbook Development (1988). Instructional materials adoption policies and procedures. Sacramento CA: California State Department of Public Instruction.

Chapter 6

Alessi, G. (1988). Diagnosis diagnosed: A systemic reaction. *Professional School Psychology,*

3(2), 145-151.

Coles, G. (1978). The learning disabilities test battery: Empirical and social issues. *Harvard Educational Review*, 48, 313-340.

English-Language Arts Curriculum Framework and Criteria Committee. (1987). English-language arts framework for California public schools kindergarten through grade twelve. Sacramento CA: California State Department of Education.

Gersten, R., Kelly, B., & Blake, G. (1991). *Coaching teachers in the effective implementation of videodisc instruction: Four case studies.* Unpublished manuscript. Eugene, OR: University of Oregon.

Goodman, K. (1969). Analysis of oral reading miscues: Applied psycholinguistics, *Reading Research Quarterly*, 5(1), 9-30.

International Institute for Advocacy of School Children; Maddalena, N., Executive chair; 296 West 8th Avenue; Eugene, OR 97401. Phone: (503) 485-6349.

Chapter 7

Arner, M. (September 8, 1988). War on 'dumb' textbooks draws publisher protests. *San Diego Tribune*.

Bateman, B. (1988). On Engelmann v. California Board of Education. *Reading Reform Foundation*.

California State Department of Education. (July 20, 1988). *English language arts SMC public input session* [Cassette]. Sacramento, CA: Author.

Curriculum Development and Supplemental Materials Commission. (1988, June). 1988 English-language arts adoption–reading. Sacramento CA: California State Department of Education.

Curriculum Development and Supplemental Materials Commission. (1988, July). Recommendations of instructional materials for adoption: 1988 English-language arts. Sacramento CA: California State Department of Education.

Engelmann, S. (1990). How sensible is your reading program? A closer look at learner verification. *Journal for Supervision and Curriculum Improvement*, 4(1), 16-22.

Engelmann v. California State Board of Education, No. 361906, (Sacramento Co. Superior Court of California, November 14, 1989).

Laufenberg, F. (Sept. 16, 1988). Letter to S. Engelmann.

Little Hoover Commission. (1989). K-12 education in California: A look at some policy issues. Sacramento, CA: Author.

Rothman, R. (November 29, 1989). Judge finds California textbook guidelines illegal. *Education Week*, 14.

Thomas, G. (1990). Let children read and teachers teach. *Journal for Supervision and Curriculum Improvement*, 4(1); 16-22.

Watkins, C. (1988). Project Follow Through: A story of the identification and neglect of effective instruction. *Youth Policy*, 7-11. July

References

Chapter 8

Brophy, J. (1986). *Teacher effects research and teacher quality.* Paper presented at the annual meeting of the American Education Research Association, San Francisco, CA.

Engelmann, S., & Carnine, D. (1990). *DISTAR Arithmetic.* Chicago, IL: Science Research Associates.

Gersten, R., Kelly, B., & Blake, G. (1991). *Coaching teachers in the effective implementation of videodisc instruction: Four case studies.* Unpublished manuscript. Eugene, OR: University of Oregon.

Grossen, B., Ewing, S., & Carnine, D. (manuscript in preparation). *The effects of considerate instruction versus the NCTM practices on the mathematics achievement of high- and low-performing sixth-graders.* Eugene, OR: University of Oregon.

Hasselbring, T., Sherwood, B., & Bransford, J. (1986). *An evaluation of the mastering fractions level-one instructional videodisc program.* Nashville, TN: George Peabody College of Vanderbilt University, The Learning Technology Center.

Hasselbring, T., Sherwood, R., Bransford, J., Fleenor, K., Griffith, D., & Goin, L. (1987-88). An evaluation of a level-one instructional videodisc program. *Journal of Educational Technology Systems*, 16(2), 151-169.

Hofmeister, A., Engelmann, S., & Carnine, D. (1985). Technology and teacher enhancement: A videodisc alternative. *Technology in Education.* Alexandria, VA: Association of Supervision and Curriculum Development.

Hofmeister, A., Engelmann, S., & Carnine, D. (1989). Developing and validating science education videodiscs. *Journal of Research in Science Teaching*, 26(7).

National Commission on Excellence in Education. (1983). *A nation at risk: The imperative for educational reform.* Washington DC: US Department of Education.

Systems Impact, Inc. (1985). *Core concepts in math and science: A series of educational videodiscs.* Washington, DC: Systems Impact, Inc., 4400 MacArthur Boulevard, N.W.

USDE-OSEP. (1985-present). Instruction leadership training in special education. Eugene, OR: University of Oregon.

Chapter 9

Floden, R. (1989). What teachers need to know about learning. In S. Gross (Ed.), *Competing visions of teacher knowledge: Proceedings from an NCRTE seminar for education policymakers: Vol 2. Student diversity* (pp. 1-38). East Lansing, MI: National Center for Research on Teacher Education.

Engelmann, S. (1989). Teachers, schema, and instruction. In S. Gross (Ed.), *Competing visions of teacher knowledge: Proceedings from an NCRTE seminar for education policymakers: Vol 2. Student diversity* (pp. 1-38). East Lansing, MI: National Center for Research on Teacher Education.

Kantrowitz, B., & Wingert, P. (1989, April 17). How kids learn. *Newsweek*, 50-57.

Kavale, K., & Forness, S. (1987). Substance over style: Assessing the efficacy of modality testing and teaching. *Exceptional Children*, 54(3), 228-239.

Resnick, L. (1988). Teaching mathematics as an ill-structured discipline. In R. I. Charles and E. A. Silver (Eds.), *The teaching and assessing of mathematical problem solving*. Hillsdale, NJ: Erlbaum and National Council of Teachers of Mathematics.

Chapter 10

Bishop, A. (1990). Mathematical power to the people. *Harvard Educational Review*, 60(3), 357-369.

Bruner, J. (1977). *The process of education*. Cambridge MA: Harvard University Press.

Engelmann, S., & Carnine, D. (1990). *DISTAR Arithmetic*. Chicago, IL: Science Research Associates.

Engelmann & Carnine v. Oregon State Textbook Commission, No. 167905976 (Lane Co. Circuit Court, June 20, 1979).

McKnight, C., Crosswhite, F. J., Dossey, J., Kifer, E., Swafford, J., Travers, K., & Cooney, T. (1987). *The underachieving curriculum: Assessing U.S. school mathematics from an international perspective*. Campaign IL: International Association for the Evaluation of Education Achievement.

National Council of Teachers of Mathematics. (1989) Curriculum and evaluation standards for school mathematics. Washington DC: Author.

National Council of Teachers of Mathematics. (1991). Professional standards for teaching mathematics. Washington DC: Author.

Piaget, J. (1969) Piaget and knowledge: theoretical foundations. Englewood Cliffs, NJ: Prentice-Hall, Inc.

Chapter 11

American Broadcasting Company. (1991). Focus-report card. *MacNeill Lehrer Report* [Television broadcast].

American Broadcasting Company. (June 6, 1991). *Prime Time Live* [Television broadcast].

American Broadcasting Company. (September, 1991). Corporate school. In *20/20* [Television broadcast].

Business Roundtable; Drew Lewis, Chair; 1615 L St. NW; Washington DC, 20036-5610.

Educational Alliance for Restructuring Now. (1991). *LEARN*. Los Angeles: Author.

Kantrowitz, B., & Wingert, P. (1991, June 17). A dismal report card. *Newsweek*, 64-66.

Mathematics Curriculum Framework and Criteria Committee. (1985) Mathematics framework for California public schools kindergarten through grade twelve. Sacramento CA: California State Department of Education.

Mathematics Curriculum Framework and Criteria Committee. (1990) Draft: Mathematics framework for California public schools kindergarten through grade twelve. Sacramento CA: California State Department of Education.

National Assessment of Educational Progress. (1991). *Report of the third national assessment*. Denver, CO: Author.

National Assessment of Educational Progress. (1989). *Reading objectives 1990 assessment*.

References

Princeton NJ: Educational Testing Service.

New American Schools Development Corporation. (1991, October). *Designs for a new generation of American schools.* Arlington, VA: Author.

Smith, J. (1991). Letter to the editor. *Educational Leadership.*

Chapter 12

Carlin v. Board of Education, Superior Court of California, County of San Diego, Case No. 303800. (1980).

National Assessment of Educational Progress. (1989). *Reading objectives 1990 assessment.* Princeton NJ: Educational Testing Service.

Office of Public Instruction. (1989). Questionnaire to teachers. Helena, Montana: Author.

Chapter 13

Apple, M. W. (1971). The hidden curriculum and the nature of conflict. *Interchange*, 2(4), 27-40.

Cuban, L. (1979). Determinants of curriculum change and stability, 1870-1970. In J. Schaffarzick & G. Sykes (Eds.), *Value Conflicts and Curriculum Issues.* Berkeley CA: McCutcheon Publishing Company.

Eisner, E. (1985). *The educational imagination: On the design and evaluation of school programs* (2nd ed). New York: MacMillan Publishing Company.

Kliebard, H. M. (1975). The rise of scientific curriculum making and its aftermath. *Curriculum Theory Network*, 5(1), 27-38.

Peters, R. S. (1959). Must an educator have an aim? In R. S. Peters *Authority, Reasonability, and Education* (pp. 83-95). London: George Allen & Unwin LTD.

Pinar, W. F. (1981). The reconceptualization of curriculum studies. In H. A. Giroux, A. N. Fenna, & W. F. Pinar (Eds.), *Curriculum and Instruction.* Berkeley, CA: McCutcheon Publishing Company.

Chapter 14

Clune, W. (1991). *Systemic educational policy.* Madison, WI: Wisconsin Center for Educational Policy.

Korol, J. (1991). *Savage inequalities.* New York: Random House.

New American Schools Development Corporation. (1991, October). *Designs for a new generation of American schools.* Arlington, VA: Author.

Shanker, A. (1990, January). The end of the traditional model of schooling—and a proposal for using incentives to restructure our public schools. *Phi Delta Kappan*, 345-357.

Chapter 15

Business Roundtable; Drew Lewis, Chair; 1615 L St. NW; Washington DC, 20036-5610.

Shanker, A. (1990, January). The end of the traditional model of schooling—and a proposal for using incentives to restructure our public schools. *Phi Delta Kappan*, 345-357.

National Council of Teachers of Mathematics. (1989) *Curriculum and evaluation standards for school mathematics*. Washington DC: Author.

National Council of Teachers of Mathematics. (1991). *Professional standards for teaching mathematics*. Washington DC: Author.

Chapter 16

Ohio State Department of Education. (1988). Section 3301.07 as amended by Senate Bill 140. In *Department of Education Regulations*.

Engelmann, S., Haddox, P., & Bruner, E. (1983). *Teach your child to read in 100 easy lessons*. New York: Simon & Schuster.

INDEX

A

A Nation at Risk – 87, 95

Abt Associates – 4-5

academic child abuse – 7-8, 68-69, 79, 82, 137, 179, 181, 194, 202-203, 205, 210-212

accountability – 63, 139, 141-143, 151, 155-157, 185-186, 196-197, 205

Achievement Goals Program (AGP) – 154, 156-160

Administrative Procedure Act (APA) – 76-77, 79-80

advanced placement – 91

Alabama – 133

Alaska, University of – 36

Alessi, Galen – 66-68

Alexander, Francie – 133, 136-137

Alexander, Lamar – 7, 138

Altwerger, Bess – 27

America 2000 – 190, 193, 202

American Express – 138

American Federation of Teachers (AFT) – 192-193

American Institute for Research in Behavioral Sciences (AIR) – 41

Anderson, Dean – 151

Anderson, Richard – 73, 75

Anti-Defamation League – 1

Apple, M. W. – 173-174

assessment – 37, 136, 139, 142, 144-146, 150, 181-184, 190-191, 193,

Association for Direct Instruction (ADI) – 209

B

Barr, Mary – 51-53

Bateman, Barbara – 79-80

Beck, Isabelle – 41, 51

Becoming a Nation of Readers – 25-27, 40-42, 51

Behavioral Analysis model – 153

Index

Bereiter-Engelmann Preschool – 1

Berman, Weiler Associates – 141

Bishop, A. – 117-118

black English – 1, 61

Bobbitt and Charters – 168-169

Boyer, Ernest – 5

Brophy, James – 90-91

Bruner, Jerome – 115-116

Buckley, Marilyn – 36-37

Bush, George – 138, 190, 193-194

Business Roundtable – 138, 140-141, 196

Bussis, A. – 51

C

California – 33-35, 40, 42, 45-46, 48, 50-51, 56, 58-59, 65, 71, 73, 75-82, 90, 100, 107, 127, 133-134, 136-137, 140-141, 143-144, 205-206, 209,

California School (of) Leadership Academy – 35, 45-46

California State Board of Education – 33-35, 71-81, 133-134, 144-145, 206-207,

California State Department of Education – 45, 74, 76, 79, 81-82, 100, 133, 206, 209

CAMPI – 160

Canada – 9, 126

Carnine, Doug – 107, 127

Center for Direct Instruction – 64

Center for the Study of Reading – 25, 73

Chernow, Dan – 42

Chicago – 142, 155, 192

Clune, William – 191-192

cognitive psychology – 100

Cognitively Oriented Curriculum – 3

computer assisted instruction – 89

Corporate School – 142

Cuban, Larry – 171-172

Curriculum Commission – 33-36, 42, 71, 74, 76, 79, 134, 137

D

developmental theory – 61, 113

Dewey, John – 60

Direct Instruction – 3-6, 40, 141, 144, 156, 156, 166

discovery learning – 3, 5, 113

DISTAR – 25, 35-36, 40-45, 97, 127-128, 157-159, 215

    Arithmetic – 97, 127

    Corrective Reading – 25

    Reading Mastery – 25, 35-36, 40-41, 71, 74-75, 215

dyslexia – 10, 211-212

E

Economic Opportunity, Office of – 1

Edelsy, Carol – 27

Education Week – 81

education, colleges of – 13, 140, 177, 187-188

Educational Imagination, The – 161, 174

Educational Leadership – 133

Educational Testing Service (ETS) – 145

    Reading Objectives – 145, 147

Eisen, Jay-Allen – 76, 81

Eisner, Elliot – 174, 176, 178

Engelmann, Siegfried – 80

English as a Second Language (ESL) – 48, 56

Estes, Dr. – 155

F

Feinberg, Janie – 64

Flesh, Rudolph – 155

Floden, Robert – 107-111

Flores, Barbara – 27

Florida – 133

Index

Follow Through – 3-6, 68, 75, 143, 153-154, 156-159, 192

Ford Foundation – 5

Foundations for Learning – 73

Framework – 36, 41-43, 65, 74, 110, 134-137

France – 113

G

Galeano, Karen – 48-50

Ginn – 154-155

Glass and House – 5

Gonzales, Phillip – 53-58, 76, 82

Goodman, Kenneth – 30-31, 61-63

Goodman, Yetta – 30-31

Grossen, Bonnie – 94

H

Hawaii – 133

Headstart – 1-3, 192

Hofmeister, Alan – 87, 97

Holt's *Biology* – 167

Hong Kong – 9, 113-114, 126

Honig, Bill – 33-34, 75-76, 81-82, 133-134, 136-138, 194

Houston – 141, 205

Hutchins, Robert – 178

I

Illinois – 146

Illinois, University of – 1, 25

individualized instruction – 172

inquiry learning – 172

Institute for Effective Education – 144

instructional design – 83, 90, 94, 100, 107

International Institute for Advocacy for School Children (IASC) – 68, 203, 210-211

International Reading Association – 4, 27, 30, 63, 146, 194

J

Japan – 9, 113-114

Journal for Supervision and Curriculum Improvement – 81-82

K

Killion, Loraine – 141

Kliebard, H. M. – 168-169

Kozol, Jonathan – 192

Kraus, Walter – 142

L

Langacker, Ronald – 28

Langer, Judith – 46-47, 51

Language and Its Structure – 28

language experience model – 5

Laufenberg, Francis, Dr. – 71, 74

Leadership Ph.D. – 178

learner verification – 33, 78-79, 134, 188

learning disabilities – 66

learning disabled – 10, 51-52, 133

learning styles – 90, 99

limited English-speaking (LES) – 48, 50-51, 53-54

Little Hoover Commission – 81

Long, James – 79

look-say basals – 62

Los Angeles Educational Alliance for Restructuring Now (LEARN) – 138, 142-144

Los Angeles Unified School District – 143

Lott, Thaddeus – 141-142

Louisiana – 133

M

MacNeil-Lehrer Report – 138

Mann, Horace – 59

metacognition – 101

Michigan – 146

Montana Office of Public Instruction – 161-162

Must an Educator Have an Aim? – 170

N

NAACP – 211

Nader, Ralph – 22

Nashville Public Schools – 93-94

Nation at Risk, A – 87, 95

National Academy of Education – 25

National Assessment Governing Board – 161

National Assessment of Educational Progress (NAEP) – 133, 194

National Center for Research on Teacher Education – 107

National Council of Teachers of English (NCTE) – 22-23, 25-27, 59, 194

National Council of Teachers of Mathematics (NCTM) – 94-95, 117-119, 126-127, 132, 145, 194, 197, 203

National Institute of Education – 25

National Science Foundation – 127

NCTM Research Advisory Committee – 117

NCTM *Standards* – 117-127, 145, 203

nested accountability – 196

New American Schools Development Corporation (NASDC) – 139-140, 144

New Zealand – 26-27

Newsweek – 133

North Carolina – 133

O

Ohio Department of Education – 209

Ohio State Board of Education – 206

Open Classroom model – 3, 5

oral reading – 199

Oregon State Textbook Commission – 127

Oregon, University of – 6, 85, 127, 177-179

Orton Society – 212

Osborn, Steve – 42, 74

P

PBS – 89

Peters, Richard – 170-171

phonics – 19, 25-26, 31, 43, 51, 73, 166, 206-209

Piaget – 3, 113, 115, 120

Pinar, William – 172

Prime Time Live – 141

Psychology Today – 101

R

Rainbow Project – 159-160

Reading Mastery – 25, 35-36, 40-41, 71, 74-75

Reading Teacher – 27

Reading Reform Foundation – 79

Reading, Center for the Study of – 25, 73

Report Card on Basal Readers – 20-22

Resnick, Lauren – 101-107, 118-119

Rio Linda, California – 143

S

San Diego – 143-144, 153-160

San Diego Tribune – 75

Sanches, Lisa – 154

Savage Inequalities – 192

schema – 101, 108, 111

schema theory – 107-109, 111-112, 115

Science Research Associates (SRA) – 35, 41, 45

Secondary School Curriculum – 116, 166-176

Shaaf, Oscar, Dr. – 127-128, 130, 132, 213

Shanker, Albert – 192-193, 196

sight basal reading programs – 60

Index

sight reading – 19

Smith, James – 133-134, 137

Smith, Robert – 157-159

sociolinguists – 1, 61

special education – 79, 99

spiral curriculum – 115-116, 125

Stanford Research Institute – 4

Stanford University – 4, 46

Systemic Educational Policy – 191

Systems Impact, Inc. – 87

T

Teach Your Child to Read in 100 Easy Lessons – 214

Tempes, Fred – 45

tenure – 177, 186

text mapping – 146, 149

Theory of Instruction – 107

Thomas, Evelyn – 128-130

Thomas, Glen – 82

Title 1 – 3, 5, 143, 192

Tucson Early Education Model – 3, 5

Twenty Questions About Teaching Language – 30, 39

20/20 – 142

U

Underachieving Curriculum, The – 113-116, 125-126

ungraded classrooms – 172

ungraded primary – 86

Urban League – 211

Utah State University – 87

V

Vanderbilt University – 93

videodisc – 6, 87, 89-95, 97

W

Walberg, Herbert J. – 155

Waters, Maxine – 73-75

Watkins, Cathy – 75

Watson, Dorothy – 20

Welsh, Lorin, Judge – 154-157, 160

Wesley Elementary School – 141-142

whole language – 3, 23-24, 26-28, 32-36, 63, 73, 86, 141, 162

ABOUT THE AUTHOR

Professor Siegfried ("Zig") Engelmann (1931-2019) combatted academic abuse of children for over 50 years.

Zig personally taught the "dyslexic" to read, the deaf to speak, and the "low performer" to outperform the "gifted." He educated the uneducable in the three Rs, and applied his genius in designing curricula that empower teachers to produce world-class students.

Zig authored more than 50 instructional programs, including *DISTAR Reading, Language*, and *Arithmetic*; *Connecting Math Concepts*; *Reasoning and Writing*; *Spelling Mastery*; and videodisc courses *Core Concepts in Math and Science*.

Before any of these programs were published, they had been tried out with children and extensively revised until they worked well for the full range of children. This unique consumer-protection model was developed by Zig and his colleagues.

Zig also wrote both professional and trade books on the theme of preventing failure through carefully designed instruction. His works include: *Teaching Disadvantaged Children in the Preschool*; *Preventing Failure in the Primary Grades*; *Give Your Child a Superior Mind*; *Your Child Can Succeed*; *Teach Your Child to Read in 100 Easy Lessons*; and *Theory of Instruction - Principles and Applications*.

War Against the Schools' Academic Child Abuse is an attempt to involve you in a campaign to protect children against irresponsible practices that lead to unnecessary failure. It's a war that Zig believed must be waged and won.

ABOUT NIFDI PRESS

The National Institute for Direct Instruction (NIFDI) is a non-profit organization focused on supporting Direct Instruction implementations with schools around the world. NIFDI also maintains a publication arm to the organization: NIFDI Press. Dedicated to publishing high quality works that support the development of effective implementations of Direct Instruction programs, the press publishes manuals and books designed to help a variety of audience purposes:

- teachers, coaches, and administrators implementing DI programs in their schools;
- parents preparing or supporting their children in academic success;
- researchers in search of theoretical and empirical studies regarding the development, efficacy and implementation of DI.

The Press also distributes other Direct Instruction and education-related titles, including:

- *Theory of Instruction: Principles and Applications*
- *Teaching Needy Kids in Our Backward System: 42 Years of Trying*
- *The Science and Success of Engelmann's Direct Instruction*
- And more!

You can order through our website at http://nifdi.org/store or by emailing orders@nifdi.org.

Made in United States
North Haven, CT
06 October 2024